FOR THE LOVE OF
CRICKET

FOR THE LOVE OF CRICKET

First published as *The Joy of Cricket* in 2014

This revised and expanded edition copyright © Summersdale Publishers Ltd, 2017

Images © Shutterstock

Summersdale Publishers Ltd
46 West Street
Chichester
West Sussex
PO19 1RP
UK

www.summersdale.com

Printed and bound in the Czech Republic

ISBN: 978-1-78685-026-3

Substantial discounts on bulk quantities of Summersdale books are available to corporations, professional associations and other organisations. For details contact general enquiries: telephone: +44 (0) 1243 771107, fax: +44 (0) 1243 786300 or email: enquiries@summersdale.com.

FOR THE LOVE OF

CRICKET

A COMPANION

GRAHAM TARRANT

summersdale

For Abigail, Francesca and Rose
– three vital extras

CONTENTS

INTRODUCTION

No other sport is as multi-faceted or as rich in history, character and drama as cricket. No other sport is as well documented or has inspired such a vast literary output. At its best it is a game of strategic complexity, subtle skill and blatant aggression – though not necessarily at the same time.

The uninitiated find the sport mystifying or dull or downright hilarious – among them the French, who sometimes claim to have invented it. But for those who love the game, whether as players or spectators or students of its history, it can be utterly absorbing and fulfilling. What other sport can be played over five fluctuating days and build to a nail-biting climax? And if you don't want to leave it so long before getting stuck into your nails, the shorter formats of the game bring their own brand of excitement.

Of course, not all Test matches and limited-overs games culminate in a gripping climax. Except for the most partisan supporters, outcomes that are too one-sided can dull the appetite, but even then there are likely to be individual performances to admire, promising newcomers to note. And if rain stops play, you can always fill in the time reading about what you're missing.

Cricket has been celebrated onstage and onscreen (the playwright Harold Pinter once referred to it as 'the greatest thing that God created on earth'), in novels and in verse – from Lord Byron to Ted Hughes. The spirit of the game (not always observed, it must be said) has been distilled as a code of conduct for life in general. As a Catholic archbishop of Liverpool once observed, 'If Stalin had learned to play cricket the world might now be a better place to live in.' (It's only fair to add that an archbishop of a rival denomination scathingly described the game as 'organised loafing'.)

Cricket, like everything else, has changed over time. In recent years, the advent of Twenty20 and the heightened profile of the women's game have created new audiences. A new generation of cricketers, players and coaches in tandem, has re-energised the sport, with faster scoring rates, improvised stroke play and innovative field placings. The game's tempo has been markedly stepped up. From the Test arena to the grass roots, cricket is on the front foot.

So what is the essence of cricket's appeal? Hopefully there are clues in the pages of this book. But one thing is very clear: our love of cricket is here to stay.

CRICKET COMES OF AGE

> **❝** *There is a widely held and quite erroneous belief that cricket is just another game.* **❞**
> **PRINCE PHILIP**

IN THE BEGINNING

The origins of cricket are lost in the mists of time. No one knows exactly how or where it all began, but by the mid-sixteenth century there is clear evidence of the game being played by children in Surrey, as recalled by a witness in a court case in 1598, looking back to his own childhood 50 years before. Also from 1598, an Italian–English dictionary compiled by John Florio refers to playing 'cricket-a-wicket'. The development of the game over the next hundred years was centred in the south-east of England – the counties of Kent, Sussex and Surrey.

Cricket's first known fatality is one Jasper Vinall, whose untimely death took place at Horsted Green, East Sussex, in 1624. He was struck on the head by the batsman, who was trying to hit the ball a second time to avoid being caught.

The English aristocracy and gentry took up the game, attracted as much by its gambling potential as by the sport itself. In the liberated years that followed the restoration of the monarchy in 1660, gambling was rife in all sports, and cricket was no exception. Wealthier patrons sponsored their own teams (often to improve their chances of winning) and employed the best exponents of the game, who became the first professional cricketers. Bats were shaped like the modern hockey stick, the curved base better able to deal with the underarm deliveries that were bowled along the ground. The wicket comprised two stumps with a single bail. Neither the batsman nor the wicketkeeper wore pads or gloves. Scorers kept a tally of the runs by making notches on a stick, every tenth notch cut larger to help with the adding up, and there were four balls to an over.

PRINCE OF CRICKET

One of cricket's foremost patrons was Frederick Louis, Prince of Wales, son of George II and heir to the throne. An occasional player of questionable skill, he captained Surrey several times and fielded his own team. The Hanover-born prince's love of sport, gambling and women endeared him to the more rakish section of society but not to his own family. There was a notable absence of grieving on their part when Frederick died in 1751 of a burst abscess in the lung, believed to have been caused by a blow from a cricket ball. Thus, England was deprived of its first cricketing monarch.

The first written laws of cricket were produced in 1744, replacing the various verbal rules of engagement that had prevailed until then. The length of the pitch was established as 22 yards (or 1 agricultural chain), unchanged to this day. Other laws drawn up by the London Star and Garter Club, whose headquarters were the Artillery Ground near Finsbury Park, included the height of the stumps, the weight of the ball, the requirement for fielders to appeal for a dismissal, and the stipulation that wicketkeepers must remain stationary and quiet until the ball has been delivered – clearly some sledging had been going on.

As the game evolved, new laws and tactics were introduced. Instead of just rolling the ball along the ground, bowlers now began to give their deliveries some air. The old style of bat was replaced by a straighter version, better suited to combatting a flighted or bouncing ball. When Thomas White of Reigate took guard with a bat wider than the wicket, the lawmakers moved in. In 1771, the width of the bat was restricted to 4 ¼ inches, still the regulation size today. Three years later the first leg before wicket (LBW) law made it into the rulebook, and soon after a third stump became mandatory.

In 1787, Thomas Lord, a Yorkshireman and a professional bowler, opened his first cricket ground at Dorset Square in Marylebone (the enterprise was underwritten by two other lords, this time of the realm). Lord fenced off the land and charged the viewing public sixpence to get in. The same year saw the formation of the Marylebone Cricket Club (MCC), which gradually took over the administration of the game. When Dorset Square became the haunt of cut-throats, Lord uprooted to St John's Wood. But his second ground was short-lived, the land being commissioned by the authorities for the construction of the Regent's Canal. In 1814, he moved again, just a few hundred yards down the road, to the site of the present Lord's Cricket Ground.

A year after its formation, the MCC revised the laws of cricket and began to assert its authority over the game. Beyond the gaze of the club's socially elite membership, cricket's rough edges would be visible for some time. But gradually, up and down the country, local enthusiasts formed their own clubs and adopted the new rules. It would be another 100 years before county cricket was properly established, but the game was taking on the shape of an organised sport.

CRICKET AT HAMBLEDON

Prior to the emergence of the MCC, the most influential cricket club in England was that of the Hampshire village of Hambledon. Run by local landed gentry who recruited the best professional cricketers, the club's ground was on Broadhalfpenny Down, opposite the Bat and Ball Inn, whose landlord Richard Nyren captained the side. Other notable players included William 'Silver Billy' Beldham, arguably the greatest batsman of the underarm era; John Small, whose own illustrious batting career spanned 40 years; and the all-rounder Tom Taylor. All are immortalised in John (son of Richard) Nyren's *The Cricketers of My Time*, the game's first literary classic.

Bowlers were becoming frustrated by the limitations of the underarm technique. None more so than John Willes of Kent, who was in the habit of getting in some batting practice with his sister Christina. Her voluminous skirt forced her to deliver the ball round-arm, which, Willes noticed, made it more difficult to play against. When, in 1822, he opened the bowling for Kent against the MCC at Lord's with a similar round-arm action he was promptly no-balled for throwing – the first in the history of the game. Other bowlers followed Willes's initiative, however, and six years later the MCC bowed to the inevitable and permitted the bowling arm to be raised level with the elbow.

By this time cricket had fanned out across the land – and across the globe, as English settlers and administrators took the game to the far-flung outposts of the British Empire and to the former colony that was now the USA, where the first official international match was played in 1844. Billed as 'United States of America versus British Empire's Canadian Province', the two-innings game at the St George's Cricket Club in New York was watched by a crowd of 10,000. Canada came out victorious in a low-scoring encounter that generated $120,000 in bets.

IT'S A FACT!

Fuller Pilch (1803–70), the greatest English batsman before the advent of W. G. Grace, revolutionised batting techniques by developing a forward defensive shot that smothered the ball before it lifted or spun. It became known as 'Pilch's Poke'.

ENTER 'THE CHAMPION'

It is impossible to overstate the impact that Dr William Gilbert Grace had on the game of cricket. An amateur with the mindset of a professional, he quite simply transformed the game. For the last 30 years of the nineteenth century he dominated the sport and in the process made himself one of the most celebrated Englishmen of all time. A native of Gloucestershire, born in the politically turbulent year of 1848, he had an imposing physique and an insatiable appetite for runs and wickets – and for sport in general. The familiar portraits of him with a long, straggly beard and portly girth, bent over a bat that seems several sizes too small, disguise the fact that he was a superb athlete. At the age of 18, having just scored an undefeated 224 for All-England against Surrey at the Oval, he left the match halfway through to compete in the national quarter-mile hurdle championship at the Crystal Palace, which he won in record time. To keep fit he ran cross-country with a pack of beagles, and he once threw a cricket ball 117 yards (107 metres). Towards the end of his cricketing days he took up bowls and for five years captained the national team.

'W. G.' didn't rewrite the record books, he created them. His amazing batting achievements were garnered on pitches that were at best unpredictable, at worst downright dangerous. Rib-crunching bouncers were mixed with deliveries that barely rose above ground level. Grace punished the short balls and unerringly blocked the shooters. Few bowlers were spared; many were afraid to bowl within his long, devastating reach. His own bowling was a medium-pace round-arm, skilfully flighted and drifting in from leg. He was a brilliant fielder anywhere, but especially off his own bowling.

He captained Gloucestershire County Cricket Club for the first 29 years of its existence, three times winning the unofficial title of Champion County, the only occasions in the club's history. His Test career spanned 20 years (13 times as captain) and started with a century, the first by an England batsman. Two of his brothers also played for their country: Dr E. M. 'The Coroner' Grace and G. F. Grace, who tragically died shortly after making his Test debut. W. G.'s commanding presence at the crease daunted bowlers and umpires alike. On one famous occasion during a minor match, having been bowled first ball, Grace calmly replaced the bail and informed the dumbstruck bowler, 'They've come to see me bat, not you bowl.' And he was right, of course. He played his last first-class game in 1908, by which time he had amassed over 54,000 runs and taken 2,800 wickets. Not bad for a man who for much of the time was a busy medical practitioner.

FIRST-CLASS RECORDS SET BY W. G. GRACE

First ever triple century (344 for MCC v Kent; a few days later he scored 318 for Gloucestershire v Yorkshire).

The first player to score 2,000 runs in a season (a feat he achieved five times).

The first to achieve 2,000 runs and 100 wickets in a season.

1871

1876

1874

The first player to perform the double of 1,000 runs and 100 wickets in a season (a feat he achieved seven times).

The first batsman to score 1,000
runs in the month of May.

|

The first batsman to make 100 centuries
(124 centuries in all). He topped 1,000 runs
in a season twenty-eight times, and nine
times took 100 or more wickets in a season.

|

1895

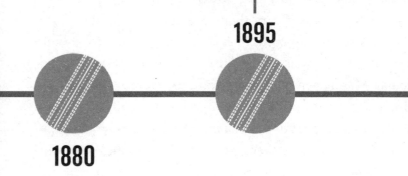

1880

|

The first England
batsman to score
a Test century
(152 v Australia
at the Oval).

THE GOLDEN AGE

The first Test between England and Australia (not yet playing for the Ashes) took place in Melbourne in 1877. Facing the very first ball in Test cricket was Australia's opening batsman Charles Bannerman, who had been born 25 years earlier in what is now the London suburb of Woolwich. He went on to score 165 ('retired hurt') and Australia won the inaugural match by 45 runs. England levelled the two-match series a couple of weeks later and sailed back to England with honours even. It was the start of a rivalry that has never lost its intensity or competitive bite.

Cricket, though restricted to the summer months, was now the most popular sport in England, drawing crowds that modern organisers can only dream about. Amateurs and professionals, who had totally separate lives and living standards off the field, played alongside each other (and in opposition in the annual 'Gentlemen v Players' fixture). County cricket was booming (the County Championship was formally constituted in 1890 as a competition between eight first-class counties; by the end of the decade there were seven more) and producing a new generation of star cricketers. The W. G. Grace era was coming to an end; in 'The Doctor's' last Test in 1899 (he was now nearly 51 years old), two future all-time greats made their international debuts: Wilfred Rhodes of Yorkshire and Australia's Victor Trumper.

IT'S A FACT!

On the last day of the Old Trafford Test in 1902, a Manchester printer, anticipating an England victory, produced a mock condolences card 'In Memory of the Australians'. The card was swiftly withdrawn from sale when news came through that Australia had won the match by three runs.

As the world moved to a new century, cricket entered its so-called Golden Age. In truth, it was probably no more 'golden' than any other age, but when viewed from the aftermath of the First World War it took on a nostalgic glow of endlessly long summers playing host to cricket matches contested in the finest spirit of the game. There was a characteristic north–south divide among the players. Yorkshire boasted the gritty, professional all-rounders Wilfred Rhodes and George Hirst (though the county was captained by the autocratic Lord Hawke). Genteel Sussex-by-the-Sea had the elegant Kumar Shri Ranjitsinhji, His Highness the Jam Sahib of Nawanagar (or 'Ranji' for short), and C. B. Fry, an all-round amateur sportsman par excellence – world record holder at the long jump, an England cap at soccer and, but for an untimely injury, an Oxford Blue at rugby. Together they piled on the runs for Sussex and England. Ranji was the first Indian to play Test cricket; Fry in later life would be offered the throne of Albania. You couldn't make it up.

Somewhere in between came Gloucestershire's Gilbert Jessop, nicknamed 'The Croucher' because of his hunched stance at the crease. Jessop was a phenomenal striker of the ball, six times getting to a first-class century in under an hour, the fastest of them in 40 minutes. In 1902, he steered England to a legendary victory against Australia, clouting a second-innings hundred in 75 minutes, just when all had appeared lost. When he was finally dismissed with 15 runs still needed to win, Wilfred Rhodes, the last man in, joined his fellow Yorkshireman George Hirst at the wicket. It is then that Hirst is said to have uttered the immortal words, 'We'll get them in singles, Wilfred.' They did get the runs (but not in singles, though the legend persists) and England were victors by one wicket.

Australia had its own stars: Clem Hill, the first player to be dismissed for 99 in a Test match (though he more than made up for it later) and the incomparable Victor Trumper, a spectacular strokemaker and the first to score a Test hundred before lunch. When Trumper died in 1915 at the age of 37, some 20,000 people lined the streets of Sydney to pay their last respects and 11 former teammates carried his coffin into the church. Archie MacLaren, one of England's premier batsmen of the time, said, 'Compared to Victor, I was a cab-horse to a Derby winner.'

Cricket had come a long way from its tentative beginnings with bat and ball. The next 100 years would see many changes to the sport and the coming and going of many great players. But it was now recognisably the game we play today.

FIELDING POSITIONS

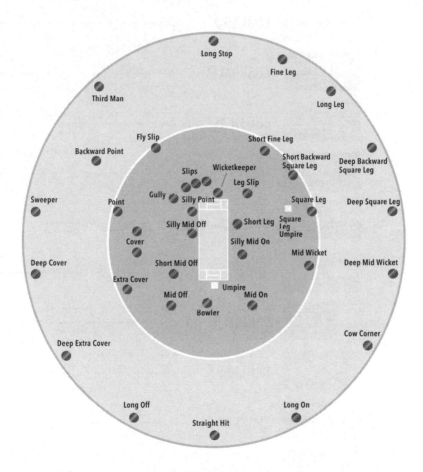

THE TEN TEST-PLAYING COUNTRIES

ENGLAND

AUSTRALIA

SOUTH AFRICA

WEST INDIES

NEW ZEALAND

INDIA

PAKISTAN

SRI LANKA

ZIMBABWE

BANGLADESH

Inaugural Test

v Australia at Melbourne, March 1877

v England at Melbourne, March 1877

v England at Port Elizabeth, March 1889

v England at Lord's, June 1928

v England at Christchurch, January 1930

v England at Lord's, June 1932

v India at Delhi, October 1952

v England at Colombo, February 1982

v India at Harare, October 1992

v India at Dhaka, November 2000

THE COUNTY CHAMPIONSHIP

County sides had been playing random fixtures against one another since the 1820s, but it was not until 1890, when the County Championship was formally established, that a proper competition structure came into being. Initially, eight counties took part: Gloucestershire, Kent, Lancashire, Middlesex, Nottinghamshire, Surrey, Sussex and Yorkshire. A year later Somerset joined the fold, and in 1895 it was the turn of Derbyshire, Essex, Hampshire, Leicestershire and Warwickshire. Worcestershire was admitted in 1899, followed by Northamptonshire in 1905 and Glamorgan in 1921. In the latter year, an invitation to enter the Championship was also extended to Buckinghamshire, but the county failed to meet the required standards for playing facilities. In 1948, Devon's application to join was declined. So the total number of counties stood at 17, until Durham made the grade in 1992.

For some it proved hard going. In 1919, when the Championship resumed after the First World War, Worcestershire's playing staff was at such a low ebb they were unable to field a side of adequate strength and opted out for the entire season. The following year the county lost three successive games by an innings and more than 200 runs. Northamptonshire went 99 matches during the period 1935–39 without a single victory. And it took Glamorgan 27 years to win their first Championship title. At the time of writing, three counties have never lifted the trophy: Gloucestershire (who were there from the start), Somerset and Northamptonshire.

Yorkshire has the most Championship titles under its belt, followed by Surrey, who won seven on the trot between 1952 and 1958. They were guided to the first five by their inspirational captain Stuart Surridge (whose family business was and is making cricket bats), the only five seasons in which he skippered the side. Fortunes change, however, and over the next 40 years the county managed to win the title only once, in 1971.

In 2000, the Championship was divided into two divisions, based on the results table of the season before. For the first six years of the new competition the bottom three counties from Division One were relegated at the end of the season and the top three from the lower division promoted. In 2006, this was changed to two up, two down. A further modification in 2017 reduced the number of teams in the premier division to eight, leaving the remaining ten counties to fight it out in Division Two.

SOME NOTABLE DATES IN CRICKET HISTORY

First Gentlemen v Players match.

Cricket is mentioned in John Florio's Italian-English dictionary, *A Worlde of Wordes*.

Thomas Lord opens what is now the current Lord's Cricket Ground.

First recorded case of an LBW dismissal (Surrey v XIII of England).

Formation of the MCC.

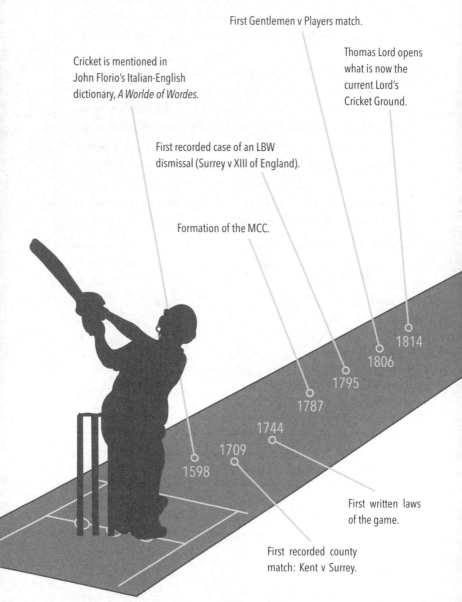

1814

1806

1795

1787

1744

1709

1598

First written laws of the game.

First recorded county match: Kent v Surrey.

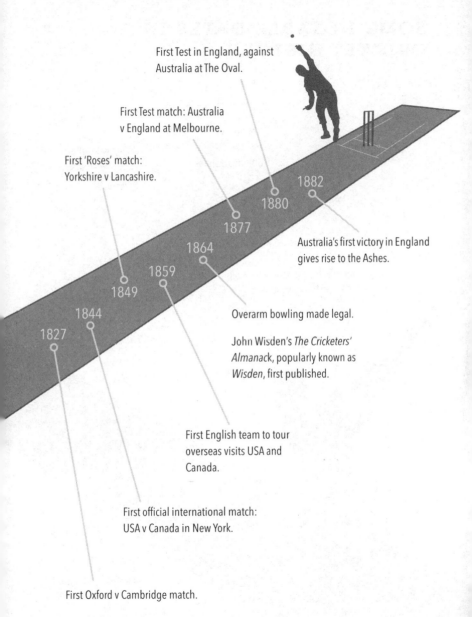

First Test in England, against
Australia at The Oval.

First Test match: Australia
v England at Melbourne.

First 'Roses' match:
Yorkshire v Lancashire.

1882

1880

1877

1864

1859

1849

1844

1827

Australia's first victory in England
gives rise to the Ashes.

Overarm bowling made legal.

John Wisden's *The Cricketers'
Almanack*, popularly known as
Wisden, first published.

First English team to tour
overseas visits USA and
Canada.

First official international match:
USA v Canada in New York.

First Oxford v Cambridge match.

SOME NOTABLE DATES IN CRICKET HISTORY

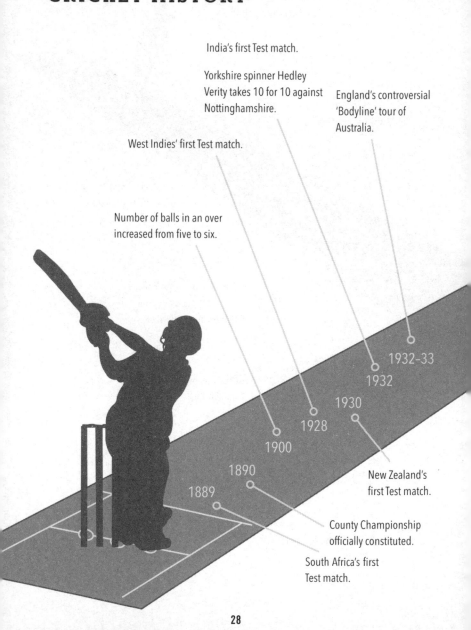

India's first Test match.

Yorkshire spinner Hedley Verity takes 10 for 10 against Nottinghamshire.

England's controversial 'Bodyline' tour of Australia.

West Indies' first Test match.

Number of balls in an over increased from five to six.

1932–33

1932

1930

1928

1900

1890

1889

New Zealand's first Test match.

County Championship officially constituted.

South Africa's first Test match.

CRICKET COMES OF AGE

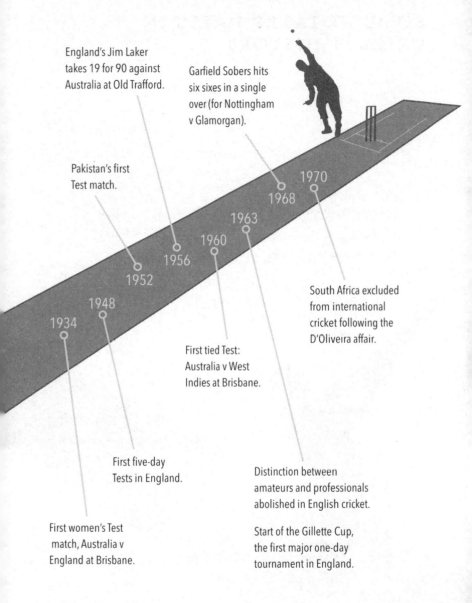

England's Jim Laker takes 19 for 90 against Australia at Old Trafford.

Garfield Sobers hits six sixes in a single over (for Nottingham v Glamorgan).

Pakistan's first Test match.

1970

1968

1963

1960

1956

1952

1948

1934

South Africa excluded from international cricket following the D'Oliveira affair.

First tied Test: Australia v West Indies at Brisbane.

First five-day Tests in England.

Distinction between amateurs and professionals abolished in English cricket.

First women's Test match, Australia v England at Brisbane.

Start of the Gillette Cup, the first major one-day tournament in England.

SOME NOTABLE DATES IN CRICKET HISTORY

Australian Graham Yallop is the first to wear a protective helmet in a Test match.

Sri Lanka's first Test match.

Centenary Test at Melbourne produces identical result to original match.

Australian media tycoon Kerry Packer launches his World Series Cricket.

The eight-ball over is abolished in Australia.

First one-day international (ODI): Australia v England at Melbourne.

1982

1980

1978

1977

1975

1973

1971

England hosts the inaugural Prudential World Cup.

First women's World Cup is staged in England.

CRICKET COMES OF AGE

Pakistan forfeits the Oval Test after being accused of ball tampering.

Andrew Strauss becomes Shane Warne's 700th Test wicket.

Alastair Cook is the youngest player to score 10,000 Test runs.

England's women become full-time professionals.

Twenty20 Cup launched in England.

Sachin Tendulkar retires from cricket after his 200th Test match.

2016

2014

2013

2007

2006

2004

2003

2000

1998

1994

1992

First ICC World Twenty20 takes place in South Africa.

Brian Lara is the first to score 400 in a Test innings (v England in Antigua).

MCC votes to admit women as members after 211 years.

South Africa's captain Hansie Cronje is banned from cricket for life after match-fixing.

Bangladesh's first Test match.

County Championship split into two divisions, with promotion and relegation.

Brian Lara scores 501 not out for Warwickshire v Durham.

Zimbabwe's first Test match.

Durham attains first-class status, the first county since Glamorgan in 1921.

GENTLEMEN V PLAYERS

The inaugural Gentlemen v Players match took place at Lord's in 1806, the 'Gentlemen' being amateur practitioners of the sport, the 'Players' being professionals. This first encounter, which the Gentlemen won, was promptly followed by another (and another victory for the Gents), before the fixture was put on hold until after the Napoleonic Wars. Indeed, it was not until 1819 that the class-divided opponents took to the field again. Thereafter the fixture became an annual event (except when there was a world war in progress), with often two, and occasionally three, matches played in a single year. Lord's, the headquarters not only of cricket but of gentleman cricketers, was the preferred venue, though other grounds such as the Oval and Scarborough (during the late-season festival) also staged matches.

The long-running fixture, predating Test matches and the County Championship, drew its last breath at Scarborough in September 1962. Out of a total of 274 games, the Players won 125, the Gentlemen 68; there were 80 draws and 1 tie. Over the years, the not-always-gentlemanly W. G. Grace scored a record 15 centuries for the amateurs, including two double hundreds. The highest individual innings by a player was 266 not out (in 1925) by one of cricket's greatest gentlemen, Jack Hobbs. Thus the distinctions were blurred. In more modern times the fixture frequently served as a Test trial, with the best talent of both persuasions on display for the selectors.

Against the background of social change that followed the Second World War, the amateur–professional divide in cricket (of which the Gentlemen v Players match was the ultimate expression) became increasingly untenable. The demarcation was at best ludicrous, at worst insulting. Some county grounds, for example, had separate dressing rooms for amateurs, even though, as happened on more than one occasion, there might be only one occupant. When playing away from home, county amateurs would be accommodated in the best hotels (all expenses paid), while the pros would stopover in B&Bs, often sharing a room to save on their meagre allowance. It all came to an end in 1963. Diehard traditionalists mourned the end of the 'Gentleman' status, believing the sport would be poorer without the amateur spirit. Professionals were content to know that from now on everyone who took to the field would simply be a player.

IT'S A FACT!

South African opener Jimmy Cook was the first Test debutant to be dismissed with the first ball of the match – against India in Durban in 1992.

RAKING OVER THE ASHES

∙∙∙

*❝ The aim of English cricket is, in fact,
mainly to beat Australia. ❞*
JIM LAKER, ENGLAND OFF-SPINNER

For English and Australian cricket followers nothing matters more
than the Ashes. The coveted trophy for which the two countries
compete represents the game at its highest level and remains
its greatest prize. The challenge, passed on from generation to
generation, has produced individual performances that have
become the stuff of legend – Laker at Old Trafford, Massie at
Lord's, Botham at Headingley, Pietersen at the Oval, Bradman
just about everywhere – and some of cricket's most dramatic
climaxes. None more so than the match that started it all.

CRICKETING MERCENARY

∙∙∙

The only cricketer to have represented both Australia
and England against each other is W. E. 'Billy' Midwinter,

a Gloucestershire-born all-rounder who played for his adopted country, Australia, in the first ever Test in 1877. He toured England two years later and was forcibly persuaded by W. G. Grace, who intercepted him at Lord's just as he was about to take to the field, to leave the touring party there and then and to come and play for his native county. Midwinter stayed with Gloucestershire for several seasons, returning to Australia as an England player in 1881–82. In all, he played eight times for Australia and four times for England, and anticipated the modern cricketing mercenary by commuting between Gloucestershire and Victoria over a number of years.

ENGLAND DEMONISED

The 1882 Oval Test match was the only one that summer and only the second played in England. There was enormous interest in the match, with 20,000 people – the largest crowd ever to attend a game of cricket – turning up on the first day. England had selected their strongest side, with the massively reassuring figure of W. G. Grace at the top of the order. All the Australians had previous Test experience, but with home advantage England were favourites to win.

On a rain-affected pitch, Australia were shot out for 63, their lowest score of the tour; but England failed to take advantage of the situation, mustering only 101 in reply. The Australian fast bowler F. R. Spofforth, whose mesmerising performances with the ball (including the first ever Test hat-trick) had won him the nickname 'The Demon', did most of the damage. An ability to generate late movement in the air and off the pitch, coupled with a deceptive change of pace, confounded the English batsmen. His 7 for 46 included the prize wicket of W. G. Grace, clean bowled for four. The pendulum swung back England's way when the opposition was dismissed in their second innings for a paltry 122. Perhaps still sore about his own cheap dismissal, W. G. resorted to an unattractive piece of gamesmanship in running out Sammy Jones when the Australian batsman momentarily strayed from his crease to pat down the pitch. It all added to the tension, but with just 85 runs needed to win, the odds were firmly with the home side.

Before taking to the field for the final innings, the irrepressible Fred Spofforth urged on his teammates: 'This thing can be done.' However, at 57 for 2, and with Grace still batting, England seemed to be coasting home. Then they hit the rocks. The man who said it could be done did it. Spofforth (bowling the mandatory four-ball overs) ripped through the England side, taking four wickets for two runs in his last 11 overs and seven wickets in all. Australia were the winners by seven runs and the Demon had match figures of 14 for 90. Cheering spectators, by no means all of them Australian, carried him shoulder high up the pavilion steps. One man stayed in his seat, dead of heart failure. One of the most exciting matches in cricket history was all over in two days.

Four days later, the *Sporting Times* published its famous mock obituary and unwittingly gave a name to cricket's most cherished trophy.

In
Affectionate
Remembrance
of
ENGLISH CRICKET,
which died at the Oval
on
29th AUGUST, 1882,

Deeply lamented
by a large circle of
sorrowing friends and
acquaintances.
RIP

N.B. – The body will be cremated
and the ashes taken to Australia.

DEMON FROM DOWN UNDER

Fred Spofforth's strikingly stern features, with a heavy black moustache and piercing dark eyes, enhanced his image as a demon fast bowler, though off the field he was an engaging character and lively raconteur. Well over 6 feet (1.8 m) tall and athletically built, he could run 100 yards (91 m) in under 11 seconds. On one occasion he made a 400-mile (644-km) round trip on horseback to play in an up-country cricket match in Australia, taking all 20 opposition wickets and all of them clean bowled.

THE URN

At the end of 1882, the Honourable Ivo Bligh (later Lord Darnley) captained the England team to Australia, with three Test matches initially scheduled. Australia won the first at Melbourne – the match originally billed as 'Mr Murdoch's Eleven v The Hon. Ivo F. W. Bligh's Team' – but England fought back to take the next two. A fourth match was then arranged, for which, bizarrely, the captains agreed to experiment by using a separate pitch for each of the four innings. Australia won.

Before leaving England the aristocratic Bligh had vowed to bring back the mythical 'ashes of English cricket'. At some point after the conclusion of the third Test (the actual details vary according to different accounts), a group of Melbourne ladies whimsically presented him with a 6-inch (15-centimetre) terracotta urn containing ashes. A red velvet bag in which to keep it came later. Attached to the urn were a few lines of doggerel clipped from a Melbourne publication, cheerfully commemorating some of the England team.

No one knows for sure what the ashes had originally been. One theory was a stump, another the outer casing of a ball. Many years later, Lord Darnley's by now elderly daughter stated that it was her mother-in-law's wedding veil that had been sacrificed. But the general consensus is that the powdery remains are most likely those of a single bail.

Despite all this, it was another 20 years before 'The Ashes' became an established part of cricket's vocabulary, *Wisden* first mentioning them by name in 1905. After Ivo Bligh's death in 1927, his widow gave the precious urn to the MCC, and it can now be seen in the museum at Lord's. Too fragile to be manhandled by victorious captains, the urn has never been used as a trophy, though a number of replicas have been held aloft for public acclamation. Since 1998, a Waterford Crystal representation of the urn has served as the official Ashes trophy.

IT'S A FACT!

Test cricket began with four balls to an over, then moved to five, then six. Several countries, most notably Australia and South Africa, increased the number to eight (England did so in 1939 but for that season only). Since 1979–80 the six-ball over has been used for all Test matches.

BODYLINE

Ashes battles have always been confrontational, sometimes ill-tempered, but only once has this historic sporting conflict turned into an international incident. On the eve of the 1932–33 tour of Australia, the England camp came up with a cunning plan to negate the run machine that was Don Bradman. Australia had won the previous series in England in 1930, with 'The Don' piling up a phenomenal 974 runs in the five Tests. He had, however, seemed uncomfortable when facing the occasional short-pitched delivery, something which England's captain Douglas Jardine now intended to exploit. With a battery of fast bowlers, spearheaded by Nottinghamshire's Harold Larwood, England would target the batsman's body, packing the leg side with fielders in close catching positions. The tactic became known as 'leg theory' or 'bodyline'.

The first two Tests passed off without major incident, England winning the first, Australia the second. In the third Test, at Adelaide, Jardine launched his bodyline attack. Australia's opener and captain Bill Woodfall was struck over the heart by a ball from Larwood, who later felled Bert Oldfield, the Australian wicketkeeper, fracturing his skull. As it happened, both deliveries had been outside the off stump, but that was not how an angry crowd saw it. And it didn't help that the autocratic Jardine appeared unrepentant.

The Australian press condemned England's tactics. Hostile cables were exchanged between the MCC and the Australian Cricket Board, and there were calls to cancel the tour. For a while diplomatic relations between the two countries were severely strained. Typical of the sombre mood was the comment by former Test cricketer Rockley Wilson, who had been Jardine's coach at Winchester: 'Well, we shall win the Ashes but we may lose a Dominion.' But order, if not peace, was restored, with England winning the Adelaide Test by 338 runs and then going on to victory in the final two matches. By the end of the year the MCC had had a change of heart and passed a resolution outlawing bodyline tactics. Australia regained the Ashes in 1934, Bradman helping himself to another 758 runs in the series.

One young Australian boy was inspired by watching Harold Larwood on the bodyline tour. His name was Ray Lindwall, and 15 years later he would wreak revenge.

IT'S A FACT!

England wicketkeeper-batsman Alec Stewart was born on 8 April 1963 (8.4.63) and scored 8,463 runs in his Test career.

WORTHY OPPONENTS

After 133 years and 325 matches fought out on opposite sides of the world, the spoils are equally divided with 32 series wins apiece and 5 drawn. Australia, however, has a significant lead in terms of match results: 130 to 106 with 89 Tests drawn.

Both countries have had periods of domination. For the first 15 years of Ashes cricket it was practically all England. Then honours were fairly even until the Bradman era, the bodyline series of 1932–33 being England's only success in almost 20 years. England finally wrested back the Ashes in the coronation year of 1953, but by the end of the decade they were once again in Australia's possession. The 1960s belonged to Australia, most of the 1970s and 1980s to England.

ASHES EXTRA

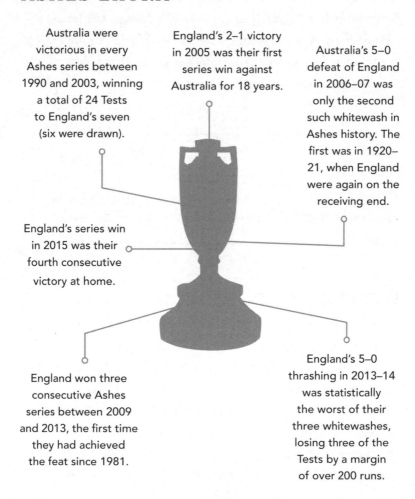

Australia were victorious in every Ashes series between 1990 and 2003, winning a total of 24 Tests to England's seven (six were drawn).

England's 2–1 victory in 2005 was their first series win against Australia for 18 years.

Australia's 5–0 defeat of England in 2006–07 was only the second such whitewash in Ashes history. The first was in 1920–21, when England were again on the receiving end.

England's series win in 2015 was their fourth consecutive victory at home.

England won three consecutive Ashes series between 2009 and 2013, the first time they had achieved the feat since 1981.

England's 5–0 thrashing in 2013–14 was statistically the worst of their three whitewashes, losing three of the Tests by a margin of over 200 runs.

THE INVINCIBLES

The Australian side that toured England in 1948 has been dubbed 'The Invincibles'. Led by the legendary Don Bradman, they remained undefeated during the five-month tour, winning 4 of the 5 Tests and 19 of the 27 other first-class matches. In most games, including the Test matches, the Australians were victors by a hefty margin. At Headingley, in the fourth Test, they were set at 404 runs in 344 minutes to win, on a pitch that was taking spin and against an England attack that included the off-spinner Jim Laker. They scored the runs with seven wickets and 15 minutes to spare. In the following Test, they dismissed for 52 an England team that included the world-class batting trio of Len Hutton, Denis Compton and Bill Edrich.

Against Essex, at Southend, they notched an astonishing 721 for 6 on the opening day. Four Australians scored centuries (Bradman himself leading the charge with 187), though the cavalier Keith Miller, disenchanted with the slaughter, allowed himself to be clean bowled first ball. To the enthusiastic crowds still undergoing rationing and other deprivations brought about by the war, the bronzed visitors from Down Under seemed like gods – and they played like them.

The side was – to any opposition – alarmingly strong in every facet of the game. In the batting department the almighty Bradman was supported by the likes of Arthur Morris, Lindsay Hassett and Neil Harvey. Ray Lindwall, Keith Miller and the big left-armer Bill Johnston led the pace attack. There was off-spin, leg-spin and the beguiling left-arm medium pace of Ernie Toshack, known as 'The Black Prince'. If there was a weakness in the line-up, England never found it. Australia were simply invincible.

TEST CRICKET TROPHIES

Trophy	Series between	First contested
The Ashes*	England and Australia	1882–83
Anthony De Mello Trophy**	India and England	1951–52
Frank Worrell Trophy	Australia and West Indies	1960–61
Wisden Trophy	England and West Indies	1963
Trans-Tasman Trophy	Australia and New Zealand	1985–86
Border–Gavaskar Trophy	Australia and India	1996–97

Southern Cross Trophy	Australia and Zimbabwe	1999–2000
Sir Vivian Richards Trophy	West Indies and South Africa	2000–01
Clive Lloyd Trophy	West Indies and Zimbabwe	2001
Basil D'Oliveira Trophy	England and South Africa	2004–05
Pataudi Trophy***	England and India	2007
Warne–Muralitharan Trophy	Australia and Sri Lanka	2007–08
Freedom Trophy	India and South Africa	2015–16
Sobers–Tissera Trophy	West Indies and Sri Lanka	2015–16
Ganguly–Durjoy Trophy	India and Bangladesh	2017

*   Essentially a symbolic trophy
**   For series played in India
***   For series played in England

MASTERS OF THEIR CRAFT

. . . .

❝ I was never coached.
I was never told how to hold a bat. ❞
SIR DONALD BRADMAN

Every era has produced its master cricketers, players who have stood at the pinnacle of the sport: W. G. Grace, Victor Trumper, Jack Hobbs, Wilfred Rhodes and Sydney Barnes, the Staffordshire bowling legend who in the years before the First World War took 189 wickets for England in 27 Tests, leading some to believe that he was the greatest bowler of them all. But in the modern game one man stands out above all others.

THE DON

The Australian Donald Bradman's first-class career lasted from 1927 to 1949. Cricketers, like anyone else, can only properly be judged in the context of their time, tempting though it is to make comparisons across different eras. Bradman is often referred to as the greatest batsman of them all, but the only thing that can be stated with absolute certainty is that he was the best of his time. That said, his statistics are unlikely ever to be equalled. In a career spanning just over 20 years he averaged 95.14 per innings; in Test matches 99.94.

Sadly, we are left with only black-and-white newsreel footage of the man in action. But what there is clearly demonstrates the Don's nimble footwork, his array of shots around the wicket (many of them unorthodox), his immaculate timing and perfect placement. Of modest height (5 foot 7 inches/1.70 metres) and build, he hit the ball with tremendous power. The runs flowed from his bat in all directions, with a speed and certainty that drove bowlers to distraction. He wasn't infallible, but he was the next best thing.

On his first tour of England in 1930, he scored a hundred in the first Test at Trent Bridge, a double century at Lord's in the next, followed by a triple century in the third Test at Headingley. In the latter match, 309 of his runs came on the first day (still a record), including a hundred before lunch; he was a month short of his 22nd birthday. Desperate to combat Bradman on the next tour Down Under, England devised the infamous bodyline theory and took the series 4–1, the Don restricted to an average of 56.57, meagre by his standards. But the triumph was short-lived. When the two sides met again in 1934 normal services were resumed, with Bradman registering another double and triple hundred in the series.

IT'S A FACT!

Don Bradman was dismissed for a duck seven times in his Test career. The Surrey and England medium-pacer Alec Bedser was the only bowler to perform the feat twice.

Don Bradman was 40 years of age when he made his fourth and final tour of England as captain of the so-called Invincibles. Like many of his contemporaries, he had lost six playing years to the war (and in his case to ill health) and was said to be past his best. Perhaps he was, but he still managed to score two Test hundreds, one of which helped steer Australia to an improbable victory at Headingley.

His final Test outing came at the Oval in a match that Australia already had in the bag, having dismissed England for 52 in their first innings. The crowd applauded him all the way to the wicket, where the England captain Norman Yardley led his team in three cheers for the Don. The second ball he received from Eric Hollies was a 'googly' and clean bowled him. Bradman was four runs short of a career Test average of 100, a statistical nicety that he was unaware of at the time. Possibly just as well.

With so much of the focus inevitably on his batting, it is easy to forget that Bradman was a brilliant outfielder (for his time) and an astute captain. Ironically, given the punishment he routinely dished out to their bowlers, the British public loved him. When he arrived in England in 1948 there were some 500 fan letters awaiting him. He personally answered every one. For fellow Australians during the economically depressed years of the 1930s he was an inspiration, drawing huge crowds wherever he went. A great ambassador for the game as well as a great player, he seldom let them down.

SOME STATISTICAL HIGHLIGHTS

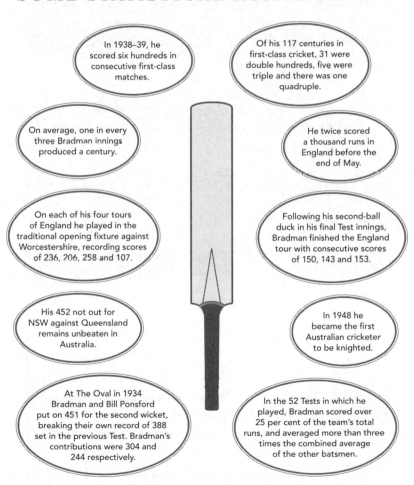

In 1938–39, he scored six hundreds in consecutive first-class matches.

Of his 117 centuries in first-class cricket, 31 were double hundreds, five were triple and there was one quadruple.

On average, one in every three Bradman innings produced a century.

He twice scored a thousand runs in England before the end of May.

On each of his four tours of England he played in the traditional opening fixture against Worcestershire, recording scores of 236, 206, 258 and 107.

Following his second-ball duck in his final Test innings, Bradman finished the England tour with consecutive scores of 150, 143 and 153.

His 452 not out for NSW against Queensland remains unbeaten in Australia.

In 1948 he became the first Australian cricketer to be knighted.

At The Oval in 1934 Bradman and Bill Ponsford put on 451 for the second wicket, breaking their own record of 388 set in the previous Test. Bradman's contributions were 304 and 244 respectively.

In the 52 Tests in which he played, Bradman scored over 25 per cent of the team's total runs, and averaged more than three times the combined average of the other batsmen.

THE DON V
SOME MODERN GREATS

		Tests	Innings	Runs	Average
Don Bradman	(AU)	52	80	6,996	99.94
Jacques Kallis	(SA)	166	280	13,289	55.37
Sachin Tendulkar	(IND)	200	329	15,921	53.78
Brian Lara	(WI)	131	232	11,953	52.88
Ricky Ponting	(AU)	168	287	13,378	51.85
Sunil Gavaskar	(IND)	125	214	10,122	51.12
Allan Border	(AU)	156	265	11,174	50.56
Vivian Richards	(WI)	121	182	8,540	50.23
Kevin Pietersen	(ENG)	104	181	8,181	47.28

IT'S A FACT!

Former England captain Ted Dexter stood as Conservative candidate for Cardiff South East in the 1964 general election but failed to dismiss the incumbent, the future Labour prime minister James Callaghan.

THE NON-DONS

While Australia boasted Don Bradman, England had its own batting giants in Wally Hammond and Len Hutton. Hammond, a professional who switched to amateur status in order to captain his country, hit 22 centuries in his 85 Tests, the highest of them 336 not out, made against New Zealand in 1933. Hutton, later England's first professional captain in modern times, boasted a record 364 against Australia at the Oval in 1938, a score that remained unbeaten for 20 years. In the Caribbean, the spectacular George Headley was known as 'The Black Bradman' (though he personally disliked the accolade), more for his prolific scoring than his batting style.

In the post-war years, other Test-playing countries began to make their mark, though Australia and England still dominated the scene. For Australia, Ray Lindwall and Keith Miller were a masterly pair of pace bowlers, while England's attack rested on the broad shoulders of the indefatigable Alec Bedser. As decade followed decade other great English players emerged: Peter May and Colin Cowdrey, Fred Trueman and Brian Statham, and the off-spinner Jim Laker, whose 19 for 90 at Old Trafford in 1956 will surely never be surpassed. Australia produced Arthur Morris and Neil Harvey and later the Chappell brothers, Ian and Greg, both successful captains of their country. From South Africa, where world-class slow bowlers have generally been in short supply, came off-spinner Hugh Tayfield; and the West Indies donated the extraordinary batting trio Everton Weekes, Frank Worrell and Clyde Walcott – 'The Three Ws' – and probably the greatest all-rounder in the history of the game, Garfield Sobers.

It was Sobers who finally overtook Len Hutton's record Test score, amassing 365 not out against Pakistan in 1958 (he followed it up with innings of 125 and 109 not out in the next Test). Later, he became the first batsman to hit 6 sixes in a single first-class over. As a left-arm bowler he possessed three equally effective styles: fast medium, orthodox spin and unorthodox spin in the form of googlies and 'chinamen'. And there has been no better close-to-the-wicket fieldsman.

SIX IN A ROW

Garry Sobers' world-record feat of hitting 6 sixes in a first-class over came in a County Championship match between Glamorgan and Nottinghamshire at Swansea in 1968. The unfortunate bowler was Glamorgan's left-arm medium-pacer Malcolm Nash. The first two balls took the aerial route over mid-wicket. The third went high over long-off. The fourth was heaved over square leg. The fifth was caught at long-off but carried over the rope by the fieldsman. The final ball of the over was deposited into the street via mid-wicket and not recovered until the next day. Seventeen years later, the Indian all-rounder Ravi Shastri equalled the feat, playing for Bombay against Baroda.

Many more great players arrived on the scene in the 1960s and 1970s – too many to include in a survey of this length. The South African Graeme Pollock (brother of fast bowler Peter and uncle to all-rounder Shaun) was the finest left-handed batsman of his time. Pakistan and India each produced a pocket-sized master opener in Hanif Mohammad and Sunil Gavaskar, respectively, while England had the inimitable Geoffrey Boycott, for so long his country's first and often last line of defence. The prolific Glenn Turner performed a similar role for New Zealand.

It was also a fertile period for spin bowlers. Derek Underwood, a deadly left-arm spinner of brisk pace (especially on rain-affected pitches), was regularly England's trump card. Slower, but no less full of guile, was the turbaned Bishan Bedi, the best of an outstanding Indian spin quartet.

From the mid-1970s to the early 1990s – their peak years – the West Indies had a superabundance of talent where it counted. A production line of lethal fast bowlers that included Andy Roberts, Joel Garner, Malcolm Marshall, Michael Holding, Curtly Ambrose and Courtney Walsh unmercifully battered the opposition. Then it was their batsmen's turn, with the explosive Viv Richards and the bespectacled powerhouse Clive Lloyd more often than not to the fore.

The new breed of wicketkeeper-batsman yielded the likes of Alan Knott, Jack Russell and Alec Stewart for England; Ian Healy and, later, Adam Gilchrist (the best of them all) for Australia; and Mark Boucher for South Africa. And if all that wasn't enough, the careers of five master all-rounders coincided: Mike Procter (South Africa), Imran Khan (Pakistan), Kapil Dev (India), Richard Hadlee (New Zealand) and Ian Botham (England).

IT'S A FACT!

Pakistan's Hanif Mohammad hit 203 not out against New Zealand at Lahore in 1965. Twenty-five years later, his son Shoaib made exactly the same score (also not out) in the first Test against New Zealand at Karachi.

As cricket moved out of the shadows of the Second World War, a new generation of world-class players lit up the scene. Here are five of the greatest.

GODFREY EVANS

The Kent wicketkeeper, unrivalled in his time, was an almost permanent fixture in the England side from 1946 to 1959. His remarkable agility belied his stocky build, lightning reflexes enabling him to pull off some stupendous stumpings and catches. He stood up to the wicket to all but the fastest bowling, a tactic that worked particularly well in partnership with England's premier strike bowler Alec Bedser, whose late swing and jagging leg-cutters Evans handled with aplomb. An ebullient character who relished the big occasion, his brilliance behind the stumps was a constant inspiration to his teammates.

As a swashbuckling lower-order batsman, Evans preferred to play an attacking role. Against India at Lord's in 1952, he missed scoring a century in a single session before lunch by just two runs. When the situation demanded, however, he could defend as well. In the 1946–47 Adelaide Test, he curbed his natural instincts in the interests of the side, taking 97 minutes to get off the mark (a record for all first-class cricket). But behind the stumps, no one was off the mark faster than Godfrey Evans.

LANCE GIBBS

The Guyanan off-spinner was the first West Indian bowler to take 300 Test wickets, and only the second from any country to achieve the feat (England's Fred Trueman being the first). Gibbs made his Test debut in 1957–58 against Pakistan, taking 17 wickets in the series. Three years later against Australia at Sydney, he took three wickets in four balls and followed this with a hat-trick in the next Test at Adelaide. For over a decade he was the spinning arm of the West Indian attack, taking five or more wickets in a Test innings no less than 18 times. His final tally of 309 Test wickets came at the staggering economy rate of 1.99 runs per over.

Gibbs' long fingers and high arm action produced exceptional turn and bounce, and his chest-on delivery and follow-through made him an exceptional fielder to his own bowling. His best Test performance was against India at Bridgetown in 1962. In the final session of a match that was heading for a draw, Gibbs took 8 wickets for 6 runs (8 for 38 overall) in a spell of 15.3 overs, 14 of which were maidens.

ALAN DAVIDSON

The New South Wales all-rounder would have thrived in today's shorter formats of the game. As it was, he thrived in the Test arena. His hostile bowling, aggressive batting and dynamic fielding made him a key member of the Australian side during the 1950s and early 1960s. His left-arm fast-medium bowling was a constant threat to batsmen, a model delivery action enabling him to move the new ball very late in the air and off the pitch in either direction. In the third over of the Melbourne Test against England in 1958–59, he removed England's top three batsmen in the space of five balls, finishing with six for the innings. Against the West Indies in 1960–61, he captured 33 wickets in just four Tests, taking 5 or more in an innings in every game.

'Davo' was a pugnacious striker of the ball who would normally bat at number 7 or 8, often changing the course of a match in a few overs of prodigious hitting. At Old Trafford in 1961, his undefeated 77 (in a last-wicket partnership of 98 with Graham McKenzie) turned impending defeat into a remarkable victory for Australia.

ZAHEER ABBAS

The bespectacled Pakistani batsman was known as 'The Asian Bradman'. He would pile on the runs with his elegant stroke play, his supple wrists despatching the ball to the boundary time and again. In 1971 at Edgbaston, in only his second Test and his first against England, he scored 274 in an innings which lasted nine hours. Three years later, in almost a repeat performance at the Oval, he notched 240. In the series against India in 1982–83, batting just once in each of the first three Tests, his scores were 215, 186 and 168. He was only the third batsman from outside England to score 100 first-class centuries (the others were Don Bradman and Glenn Turner) and the first Pakistan cricketer to pass 4,000 runs in Tests.

For 13 years as a member of the Gloucestershire side Zaheer plundered county bowling attacks, totalling 1,000 runs in a season ten times and twice topping 2,000. On eight occasions he scored a century in each innings of a match – a world record. Even more remarkably, four of these were a double and single hundred in the same game, and all of them not out.

BARRY RICHARDS

As a result of South Africa's banishment from international cricket between 1970 and 1991, Barry Richards' Test career was limited to four matches, in two of which he scored centuries – a clear sign of what the cricket world would be missing. From that point on, the prolific right-hand opening batsman would divide his time and talent between the domestic competitions of England, Australia and his home country. For Hampshire in the 1970s his spectacular opening partnerships with West Indian Gordon Greenidge made a mockery of apartheid and most bowling attacks. An excellent judge of line and length, equally strong off the front or back foot, Richards made batting look easy. He could play every shot in the book, combining elegant stroke play with raw power.

Playing for South Australia in 1970–71, he averaged 109.85 for the season. He took 224 and 146 off the MCC touring side in successive games against them, and in the same year scored a career-best 356 against Western Australia (325 of them in a single day). Deprived of challenges at the highest level, Richards could sometimes become bored and careless at the crease if not fully tested. But that was the most opposing bowlers could hope for!

CARIBBEAN KNIGHTS

Eleven West Indian Test cricketers have been knighted to date, outnumbering those of any other country. On paper they make a world-beating team:

(Batting order)
Sir Conrad Hunte (Barbados)
Sir Richie Richardson (Leeward Islands)
Sir Viv Richards (Leeward Islands)
Sir Everton Weekes (Barbados)
Sir Clyde Walcott (Barbados)
Sir Frank Worrell (Barbados), captain
Sir Garfield Sobers (Barbados)
Sir Learie Constantine (Trinidad)
Sir Andy Roberts (Leeward Islands)
Sir Wes Hall (Barbados)
Sir Curtly Ambrose (Leeward Islands)

The four-man pace attack of Ambrose, Hall, Roberts and Constantine would destroy most batting line-ups, with Sobers able to provide variation with his mixture of spin and medium pace. The West Indian batsmen would wield their own form of destruction. Walcott, who started out as a wicketkeeper, would don the gloves.

Constantine (the only pre-war player in the side and later elevated to the peerage) was knighted as a politician and diplomat, rather than for services to cricket. But, a brilliant all-rounder in his day, he is well worthy of inclusion.

The twenty-first century is still in its infancy and will doubtless produce many great cricketers of its own. Here are some recent masters of their craft.

BRIAN LARA

In 1994, within the space of two months, Trinidad's most famous son broke two world records: the highest score in a Test match (375 against England in Antigua) and the highest in any first-class game (501 not out for Warwickshire against Durham at Edgbaston). He notched 34 Test centuries in all and a further 19 in ODIs. As the West Indies side declined on whole, Lara increasingly played a lone hand. In the 2001–02 series against Sri Lanka, he scored 42 per cent of the team's runs, with a personal tally of 688. Australia's Matthew Hayden eclipsed Lara's record Test score, but not for long. Within six months Lara had reclaimed the top spot with an innings of 400 not out against hapless England.

At his best, and he frequently was, Lara was a batsman of breathtaking brilliance. But the pressures that came with success and the strain of propping up a weak West Indian side (much of the time as captain) took their toll. Acrimonious disputes with the administrators added to his problems and accelerated his departure from the game.

SHANE WARNE

In his first Test for Australia, against India at Sydney in 1992, Shane Warne's bowling stats were 1 for 150 (Sachin Tendulkar had figures of 1 for 2 in the same match, but he bowled 44 fewer overs). But shrewd judges, among them former Australian captain Richie Benaud, himself an eminent leg-spinner, had spotted something very special about the chubby, blonde Victorian. The legendary delivery that bowled Mike Gatting a year later made their point.

Warne's craftily concealed spinning options bamboozled the best batsmen around, sometimes embarrassingly. He made leg-spin fashionable. Warne was forced to change his bowling action after a shoulder operation in 1998, and taking forbidden substances (allegedly in the form of a diuretic to help reduce weight) cost him a year's ban in 2003. But the irrepressible Warne bounced back and carried on where he had left off. He became the first bowler to take 600 Test wickets, then 700. He recorded one Test hat-trick but might have had several more. He rarely had an off day, and if he did the opposition would pay for it later. Behind the razzamatazz was a wily cricket brain, and there was no fiercer competitor.

IT'S A FACT!

West Indian batsman Chris Gayle was the first cricketer to hit a six off the opening delivery of a Test match. He performed the feat against Bangladesh in 2012, in Test number 2,051.

GLENN McGRATH

Glenn McGrath was selected for his country after playing in only eight first-class matches. It was the beginning of a Test career that would span 13 years, during which he became the first fast bowler to be capped 100 times by Australia. His haul of 563 Test wickets comfortably passes the previous record set by a 'quickie' (Courtney Walsh, 519) and places him fourth in the rankings behind his three great spinning contemporaries – Muttiah Muralitharan, Shane Warne and Anil Kumble.

Only Dennis Lillee can challenge him as the greatest Australian fast bowler of the modern era, possibly of all time. McGrath's metronomic line and length on or about the off stump, and his ability to extract extra bounce from all but the flattest pitches, troubled every batsman who faced him. He was equally effective in ODIs and is the leading wicket-taker in the history of the Cricket World Cup. He retired from the game at the end of the 2007 competition, but not before he was adjudged 'Man of the Tournament'.

SACHIN TENDULKAR

As a 14-year-old schoolboy, Sachin Tendulkar shared a record unbroken partnership of 664 with his friend Vinod Kambli, who would follow him into the Indian team. At 15 and a half he became the youngest cricketer to score a century on his first-class debut. He made his first Test hundred at the age of 17 and had another 15 under his belt before he was 25. The runs never stopped flowing: 51 Test centuries in all, another 49 in ODIs, including the first ever double hundred in the shorter format. Bowing out in his 200th Test was yet another statistical milestone.

Tendulkar has been to the modern game what Bradman was in a previous era: put briefly, a nightmare for bowlers. Near technically perfect, adept on any surface and with every shot in the book, he had a hunger for runs that sapped the strength of bowling attacks around the world. The Indian crowds worshipped him. A lesser man would perhaps have wilted under the steamy adoration, but like a prize hothouse bloom, Tendulkar seemed to thrive on it.

MUTTIAH 'MURALI' MURALITHARAN

Murali's bowling action has been a mixed blessing. Shaped by a deformed elbow, his unusual style of delivery helped to confound batsmen while at the same time attracting accusations of throwing. With his rapid wrist movement he extracted more turn than most off-spinners, but it was not until he developed his *doosra* – a ball that turned the other way or held its line – that he really came into his own. In the 1995 Boxing Day Test, Australian umpire Darrell Hair no-balled him for throwing seven times in three overs. Three years later fellow umpire Ross Emerson repeated the call. Murali's bowling action was scrutinised on film by the authorities and pronounced legitimate, though the debate continued throughout his career.

He overtook Shane Warne's 708 wickets, finishing with a symmetrically satisfying 800, garnered in 12 Tests fewer than his rival (though he did bowl over 3,000 balls more). There were a further 534 wickets in ODIs. Despite often being the only Tamil in the Sri Lankan side during years of bloody ethnic conflict, Murali remained his country's most popular and revered cricketer.

JACQUES KALLIS

Jacques Kallis may have lacked the charisma of Shane Warne or the god-like status of Sachin Tendulkar, but he was not short of much else. The most outstanding all-rounder in recent times, he compiled over 13,000 runs in Tests before retiring from first-class cricket in 2013, and a further 11,500 in ODIs. His Test batting average of 55.37 is up there with the very best, and his tally of 45 Test hundreds (the last of them coming on cue in his final match) is second only to Tendulkar's. In 2010, at the age of 35 and when most cricketers' glory days are behind them, he scored his maiden Test double hundred and two years later followed it up with another.

His fast-medium bowling predictably slowed down in the later years, though he could still surprise batsmen with a sudden fast ball or some extra bounce. His 565 wickets for South Africa were almost equally divided between Test matches and ODIs (with a few Twenty20 victims on top of that). And if all that wasn't enough, he pocketed 200 Test catches – the second highest on record.

MASTER BLASTERS

As the game has quickened in tempo, more master blasters have appeared on the scene: Ben Stokes (England), David Warner (Australia), Chris Gayle (West Indies), Brendon McCullum (New Zealand) and M. S. Dhoni (India) among the international stars. Spectacular bouts of hitting have become the norm, especially in the Twenty20 format. South Africa's AB de Villiers registered the fastest ever century in international cricket, in an ODI against the West Indies in 2015. His hundred came up in 31 balls, breaking New Zealander Corey Anderson's record of the year before by five balls. In Test cricket, Brendon McCullum (New Zealand) holds the record for the fastest Test century (54 balls), Nathan Astle (New Zealand) for the fastest double hundred (153 balls), with Virender Sehwag (India) the fastest to 300 (278 balls).

GETTING PHYSICAL

...

> ❝ *I would have died for Yorkshire.*
> *I suppose once or twice I did.* ❞
> **BRIAN CLOSE, FORMER YORKSHIRE CAPTAIN**

LATE STARTERS AND FINISHERS

The oldest cricketer to make his Test debut was James Southerton, who was 49 years and 119 days old when he played for England in the inaugural match at Melbourne in 1877. Three years later he became the first Test cricketer to die, falling ill with pleurisy. Since Test matches were not officially designated as such until much later, the significance of his early demise escaped the unfortunate Southerton.

An off-break bowler who switched from round-arm to overarm, Southerton played for Surrey, Sussex and Hampshire – sometimes, in the days before birth and residential qualifications, in the same season. Although he was 32 before he took a wicket in first-class cricket, his seasonal tally exceeded 100 wickets on ten occasions. In 1869, in a match against Lancashire, he became the first bowler to take four wickets in five balls.

Once, when batting, he believed that he was out caught and 'walked'. The fielding side sportingly insisted that the catch had not been made, but Southerton refused to change his mind. His dismissal was recorded in the scorebook:

J. Southerton, retired, thinking he was caught, 0

The great Yorkshire all-rounder Wilfred Rhodes is the oldest cricketer to have played in a Test match. He was 52 years and 165 days old when he made the last of his 58 Test appearances for England in 1930. Rhodes also holds the record for the longest Test career, just short of 31 years, during which time he scored 2,325 runs and captured 127 wickets.

IT'S A FACT!

The Lancashire all-rounder R. G. 'Dick' Barlow, who played 17 times for England and took part in the 1882 Test match that gave rise to the Ashes, died in 1919. The inscription on his tombstone reads: 'Bowled At Last'.

The oldest Australian to play Test cricket (and the second oldest overall) was Bert Ironmonger, a left-arm spinner whose bowling action was considered questionable in some quarters. As a child he had lost the top joint of his forefinger in a chaff-cutter on the family farm and learned to spin the ball off the remaining stump. A less-than-agile, thick-set figure, nicknamed 'Dainty' by his teammates, Ironmonger was a liability in the field but a very effective wicket-taker, his 74 Test dismissals costing less than 18 runs apiece. He made his first Test appearance in 1928 at the age of 46 (he claimed to be 41 at the time) and his last a month short of his 51st birthday. His prowess with the ball was not matched by his batsmanship. The story goes that on one occasion his wife telephoned him at the Melbourne ground only to be told that he had just gone in to bat. 'Don't worry,' she replied, 'I'll hang on.'

LATE STARTER

In 1950, at the age of 72, Raja Sir Maharaj Singh, captaining the Bombay Governor's XI in a three-day match against a touring Commonwealth XI, became the oldest cricketer to make his first-class debut and the oldest to play in any first-class match. In his one innings, batting at number 9, he was dismissed for four runs off the bowling of Jim Laker. The age difference between batsman and bowler was a trifling 44 years. After his brief appearance on the opening day – the extent of his first-class career – Singh played no further part in the game, handing over the captaincy to the younger and even more grandly titled Maharaja of Patiala, a veteran of 50 first-class matches, including one Test cap.

YOUNG BEGINNERS

The youngest Test debutant on record is Pakistan's Hasan Raza, who was allegedly 14 years and 227 days old when he appeared against Zimbabwe at Faisalabad in October 1996. Subsequent doubts were raised about his date of birth, leaving some uncertainty as to his exact age at the time, which is now thought to have been closer to 15. Despite an impressive record in domestic cricket the gifted Hasan Raza played in only seven Tests, with a top score of 68.

Most of the 50 youngest Test cricketers on record herald from the Indian subcontinent, those from Bangladesh joining the ranks of Indians and Pakistanis. Sachin Tendulkar was only 16 when he made his Test debut in 1989, losing his wicket to Waqar Younis, who was little more than a year older. Cricketers from other parts of the world generally take longer to mature, or at any rate to make it into the Test arena. Among the rare exceptions have been the West Indies' Garry Sobers and Australia's Ian Craig, both only 17 when they first represented their countries in the 1950s, and New Zealand's Daniel Vettori, who was 18. England's youngest capped player remains, after nearly 70 years, Yorkshire's Brian Close, who made his Test debut in 1949 against New Zealand at the age of 18 years, 149 days.

IT'S A FACT!

Pakistan's Sajjida Shah is the youngest cricketer of either sex to have played international cricket. She made her debut in an ODI against Ireland five months after her twelfth birthday, and was in the Test side a week later.

SOMETHING TO OVERCOME

Some Test cricketers have succeeded despite having to overcome long-term disabilities of one sort or another.

'TIGER' PATAUDI

The Nawab of Pataudi, Jr (his father, the senior Nawab, played for England in the 1930s), later known as Mansur Ali Khan, was involved in a car accident in 1961 while at Oxford, which left him almost blind in one eye. An immensely promising career seemed to be at an end. But 'Tiger' Pataudi was made of stern stuff and within a month was back in the nets, adjusting his stance to cope with the impaired vision. He went on to captain India in 40 of his 46 Tests (in which he scored six centuries) as well as leading Sussex, for whom he played for a number of years.

BHAGWATH CHANDRASEKHAR

The Indian leg-spinner Bhagwath Chandrasekhar contracted polio at the age of five, leaving him with a withered right arm, which remarkably became his bowling arm later in life. If anything, the wasted limb aided his delivery of googlies, fizzing top-spinners and sharply turning leg-breaks. He used his left arm for fielding. 'Chandra' took over a 1,000 wickets in first-class cricket, 242 of them in Tests. None were more important than his 6 for 38 at the Oval in 1971, when England were brushed aside for 101 to give India their first series victory against the home side.

ATHOL ROWAN

South Africa's Athol Rowan sometimes bowled his off-breaks with his left leg in an iron brace. The leg, damaged by a wartime explosion in the Western desert, was often very painful, and the bowler was unable to put his full weight on the front foot. Despite this, Rowan played in 15 Tests (his brother Eric also represented his country) and was one of the best post-war spin bowlers produced by South Africa. He dismissed the great Len Hutton 11 times, 5 times during the 1948-49 series, for which feat alone he deserves to be remembered.

> ## IT'S A FACT!
>
> Athanasios John Traicos, the only Egyptian-born Test cricketer, played for South Africa three times in 1969–70. His next Test appearance was for Zimbabwe in 1992 – an interval of 22 years and 222 days, the longest on record.

DIRK WELLHAM

Dirk Wellham, who scored a century on his Test debut for Australia against England at the Oval in 1981, suffered from diabetes and had to take regular insulin shots. Wellham, whose sole three-figure score this was in his six-Test career, had been stranded on 99 for 25 minutes, during which time he was dropped by Geoffrey Boycott.

LEN HUTTON

After the war, England's premier batsman Len Hutton returned to cricket with his left arm 2 inches shorter than the right. A fall in the gym (Hutton had been a sergeant-instructor in the Royal Army Physical Training Corps) had fractured his forearm, and two operations, including a bone graft, were required to repair the damage. The injury continued to trouble Hutton for the rest of his career and, no longer able to fully rotate his wrists, he dropped the hook shot from his repertoire. Nevertheless, until his retirement from Test cricket in 1955, he remained the batsman opposition bowlers most wanted to dismiss.

TONY GREIG

Tony Greig was 14 when he had his first epileptic fit. The South African–born former England captain controlled the condition through medication for the rest of his playing career, at the time one of the best-kept secrets in the game. Appearing for Eastern Province in 1971–72, he experienced an epileptic seizure while on the field and had to be held down by his teammates. The official explanation was heatstroke. A charismatic and sometimes controversial leader and an outstanding all-rounder, Greig played 58 times for England, taking 141 Test wickets and averaging over 40 with the bat.

ELEVEN POST-WAR BESPECTACLED TEST CRICKETERS
(other than Geoffrey Boycott)

....

Eddie Barlow (South Africa) – opening batsman
Dilip Doshi (India) – slow left arm

Walter Hadlee (New Zealand) – batsman

Clive Lloyd (West Indies) – batsman

Norman 'Tufty' Mann – slow left arm

M. J. K. Smith (England) – batsman

David Steele (England) – batsman

Alf Valentine (West Indies) – slow left arm

Daniel Vettori (New Zealand) – slow left arm

Dirk Wellham (Australia) – batsman

Zaheer Abbas (Pakistan) – batsman

KEEPING FIT

The county cricketer of earlier decades paid scant regard to fitness, beyond the bare necessities. Many players smoked, and it was not unusual to see a cricketer downing a pint of beer during the tea interval. One former England captain, Freddie Brown (admittedly an amateur), had been known to have a gin and tonic brought out to him in the field, though not when on Test duty. Nowadays, the professional cricketer's body, if not a temple, is a fortress, built to withstand the onslaughts of the modern game.

Keeping fit is also essential for the average club cricketer, even if not pursued to the same extremes. Running, skipping or cycling, along with a prescribed regime in the gym, improves stamina and keeps the weight down.

Exercises such as press-ups, pull-ups, deadlifts and squats will help tone the muscles, ease the joints and strengthen the legs, back and shoulders. Bending forward from the hips, swivelling the head and shoulders, and touching your toes from a sitting or standing position will improve mobility. Swinging a bat with each arm in turn or running with your pads on are other useful exercises.

Unless you are in excellent shape to begin with, it's important to build up these activities in a measured way, seeking out expert advice if need be. Rushing at things can do more harm than good. A sensible diet is also important.

IT'S A FACT!

The Australian captain Warwick Armstrong, who led his side to a 5–0 whitewash over England in 1921, weighed 140 kilos (22 stone). His nickname was 'The Big Ship'.

TEST CRICKETERS' HEIGHT CHART

IMPOSINGLY TALL

7 ft 1 in. (2.15 m)   Mohammad Irfan (PAK)

6 ft 8 in. (2.03 m)   Joel Garner (WI)
Bruce Reid (AUS)
Boyd Rankin (ENG)

6 ft 7½ in. (2.02 m)   Tony Greig (ENG)

6 ft 7 in. (2.01 m)   Tom Moody (AUS)
Curtly Ambrose (WI)
Chris Tremlett (ENG)
Stephen Finn (ENG)
Sulieman Benn (WI)
Jason Holder (WI)

6 ft 6 in. (1.98 m)   Jacob Oram (NZ)
Abey Kuruvilla (IND)

IMPRESSIVELY SHORT

5 ft 5 in. (1.65 m)	Tatenda Taibu (ZIM)
	Sachin Tendulkar (IND)
5 ft 4 in. (1.62 m)	Alvin Kallicharran (WI)
	David Williams (WI)
5 ft 3 in. (1.6 m)	Gundappa Viswanath (IND)
	Mushfiqur Rahin (BAN)
	Parthiv Patel (IND)
5 ft 2 in. (1.57 m)	A. P. 'Tich' Freeman (ENG)
5 ft (1.52 m)	Walter 'Tich' Cornford (ENG)

IT'S A FACT!

On the 1982–83 tour of Australia, England players Derek Randall and Eddie Hemmings were moved into a room together after their original room-mates complained about their snoring.

GETTING EQUIPPED

Changing clothes

The eighteenth-century cricketer wore a frilly shirt, breeches, silk stockings and buckled shoes and sported a three-cornered hat. In time, trousers, held up by braces or a wide belt with a metal clasp, replaced the breeches. A tall hat (black or white) became the regulation headgear and, on the shirt front, out went the frills and in came the bow tie. The cap, sweater and blazer comprised the next sartorial step change, with boots replacing shoes. Until the last quarter of the twentieth century the most visible changes to a cricketer's appearance were more likely to do with facial hair. Everything else remained pretty much the same – until the advent of the helmet and coloured clothing.

Gloves and pads were improved over the years, but apart from the abdominal guard ('box') the batsman had no other protection than his bat. Wicketkeepers would often line their own gloves with raw meat to safeguard their hands. In contrast, the modern cricketer's body armour includes a thigh guard, chest guard, elbow guard and arm guards, as well as the ubiquitous helmet and visor. When standing up to the stumps, many wicketkeepers now wear safety glasses behind their helmet grill for additional protection.

Choosing the right gear

Bat

Choose a bat that is the correct size and weight for you and has a handle the right length. Put it through its paces before making a purchase. A good test is to hold it straight out in front of you, at eye level, to make sure it is not too heavy.

Batting gloves
They should fit as well as ordinary gloves, giving you a perfect grip on the handle. If your hands are inclined to sweat, invest in gloves that have absorbent palms.

Pads
Make sure the pads are the right thickness and height, especially when it comes to the knee roll. Lighter pads may give you better mobility, but protecting your shins and knees is a more important factor. For wicketkeepers, on the other hand, lighter pads are generally the better option.

Helmet
This has to sit comfortably on the head without restricting your movement in any way. If it has a grill, check that you have adequate visibility and that the gap between the peak and the top of the grill is sufficiently narrow to stop a ball getting through – equally important for wicketkeepers and close fieldsmen in the line of fire.

Wicketkeeping gloves
The gloves should be large enough to protect the wrists. You can wear an extra pair of inner gloves if it feels more comfortable that way.

Abdominal guard
Should be worn not only when batting but also behind the stumps or when fielding close to the wicket. Even then, it can hurt!

FAMILY CONNECTIONS

CRICKETING DYNASTIES

Cricket has always been a family sport, played by fathers and sons, brothers and – now more than ever – sisters. At the first-class level of the game, there are notable instances of the cricketing gene spanning several generations.

THE COWDREYS

In 1926, Ernest Cowdrey, an English tea-planter in India, made his one and only first-class appearance: for the Europeans, a team which competed in the Bombay tournament. When his son was born eight years later, Ernest had him christened Michael Colin, ensuring that he would share the most famous initials in cricket. The gesture wasn't wasted. Colin Cowdrey became one of England's most celebrated cricketers, playing in 114 Tests (he was the first player from any country to make 100 Test appearances), 27 of them as captain. He scored 22 Test centuries and held a record number of catches (120), most of them in the slips. He led his county, Kent, for 15 years. In 1997 he was made a life peer.

Chris Cowdrey followed in his father's footsteps without ever filling them. An accomplished all-rounder, he skippered Kent for a number of seasons and won six Test caps, one of them as a stop-gap captain. His younger brother Graham, a hard-hitting, middle-order batsman, also turned out for Kent, making 179 appearances for the county. A fourth-generation Cowdrey – Fabian, son of Chris – made his debut for the family county in 2013. He has a lot to live up to.

THE D'OLIVEIRAS

Basil D'Oliveira was a *cause célèbre*. Born in South Africa as a 'Cape Coloured', he was debarred by the authorities from playing cricket at the higher levels of the sport, despite his exceptional talent. Supporters of his cause, notably the broadcaster John Arlott, arranged a contract with one of the Lancashire League sides which enabled D'Oliveira to come to England. He joined Worcestershire in 1964 and made it into the England side two years later. An outstanding all-rounder, D'Oliveira won 44 Test caps and would undoubtedly have added to that tally had he not been well into his 30s when he made his debut. As it was, he continued to turn out for his county until he was nearly 50. His inclusion in the England side selected to tour his homeland in 1968 led to South Africa's exile from international cricket – a story that is told in chapter seven of this book.

As a regular member of the Worcestershire side from 1982 to 1995, Basil's son Damian D'Oliveira helped the county to win two Championship titles. A reliable middle-order batsman, his highest score was 237. His son Brett made his debut for the county in 2012. Four years later, his score of 202 not out against Glamorgan made history. Following grandfather Basil and father Damian, he was the third generation to score a first-class double century – a unique feat.

IT'S A FACT!

Australian wicketkeeper-batsman Alyssa Healy is married to fast bowler Mitchell Starc and is the niece of former wicketkeeper, now TV commentator, Ian Healy.

THE HEADLEYS

From 1929, for almost 20 years, George Headley was the standout batsman for the West Indies and one of the greatest ever. He scored ten centuries in his 22 Tests, finishing with a batting average of over 60. A batsman with Caribbean flair, he would flail opposition bowling attacks, scoring his runs quickly and to all parts of the ground. In one period he went ten years without missing a Test.

Ron Headley, son of George, played most of his cricket for Worcestershire, for several years opening the innings with New Zealand batting star Glenn Turner. In 1973, he was drafted into the injury-hit West Indies side on tour in England and played in two Test matches, but without distinction.

Third-generation Dean Headley broke the family mould, opting to become a fast-medium bowler. He played for Kent and later Middlesex, and 15 times for England during the late 1990s. His best Test performance was 6 for 60 in Australia's second innings at Melbourne in 1998–99, paving the way for an England victory by 12 runs. The Headleys remain the only family to have produced three generations of Test cricketers.

THE HUTTONS

Yorkshireman Len Hutton (later Sir Leonard) made an inauspicious start to his Test career, scoring zero and one against New Zealand in the opening match of the 1937 series. Fortunately for him (and for England), the selectors kept faith with the 21-year-old, who repaid them in the next Test by scoring a century. From then on, until his retirement 18 years and 77 Tests later, Hutton was almost a permanent fixture in the England side. Denis Compton apart, he outclassed all other English batsmen. As captain, in the Coronation year of 1953, he led England to one of their most celebrated Ashes victories, earning the gratitude of the nation.

Following his illustrious father was never going to be easy for Richard Hutton. A good county all-rounder (a fast-medium bowler and useful lower-order batsman), he played for Yorkshire for 12 years and for England five times. His inclusion in the Test side, however, smacked of wishful thinking on the part of the selectors. Richard's son Ben made his debut for Middlesex in the late 1990s as a top-order batsman and occasional seam bowler. After a couple of successful seasons with the bat he was appointed Middlesex captain in 2004, but plagued by illness he dropped out of the side and announced his retirement from cricket three years later.

THE PARKS

Jim Parks was a Sussex all-rounder (opening bat and a medium-pace bowler) for 15 years before the Second World War. In 1937 he set a record that is never likely to be equalled, scoring 3,003 runs (including 11 centuries) and taking 101 wickets in the season. Unsurprisingly, he was selected for England that year, but only played the one Test. He shared most of his time at Sussex with his younger brother Harry, a fellow batsman who scored 42 first-class hundreds (one more than Jim).

Jim Parks, Jr started out as a specialist batsman, following his father and uncle into the Sussex side. He was first picked for England in 1954 against Pakistan, but it wasn't until he took up wicketkeeping duties some years later (by chance when the regular county stumper was injured) that his international career took off. He played 46 Tests in all, most of them in the 1960s. At the end of his career he spent three fruitful years with Somerset.

Like his father, Bobby Parks earned his living behind the stumps. He never won a Test cap, though he did keep wicket for England for a few hours against New Zealand at Lord's in 1986, as a substitute for an injured Bruce French. His 13-year county career was split between Hampshire and Kent.

THE TREMLETTS

Maurice Tremlett burst onto the scene in 1947, taking eight wickets on debut for Somerset against Middlesex at Lord's.

He played three Tests in the Caribbean the following winter but never fulfilled his early promise, and his bowling skills increasingly deserted him. He focused on his batting and became a consistent performer in the middle order for Somerset and, in 1956, the county's first professional captain. The baton was passed on to his son Tim, a key member of the Hampshire side during the 1980s. A steady medium-pace bowler and useful lower-order batsman, he played over 200 matches for the county.

Chris Tremlett (Hampshire and Surrey) was third in line and the most successful at international level. At his best and when fully fit, he could be a devastating fast bowler. He played 12 Tests and 15 ODIs for England, peaking on the 2010–11 Ashes tour when he took 17 wickets in three Tests, helping England to their first series victory Down Under for 24 years. Back problems and other injuries interrupted his career and, although he returned to the England side, he never recovered his best form.

FATHER AND SON TEST CENTURIONS

Father	Son
Lala Amarnath, India (1)	Surinder Amarnath, India (1)
	Mohinder Amarnath, India (11)
Chris Broad, England (6)	Stuart Broad, England (1*)

Walter Hadlee, NZ (1)   Richard Hadlee, NZ (2)

Rod Latham, NZ (1)   Tom Latham, NZ (5*)

Vijay Manjrekar, India (7)   Sanjay Manjrekar, India (4)

Geoff Marsh, Australia (4)   Shaun Marsh, Australia (3*)

Hanif Mohammad, Pakistan (12)   Shoaib Mohammad, Pakistan (7)

Nazar Mohammad, Pakistan (1)   Mudassar Nazar, Pakistan (10)

A. W. 'Dave' Nourse, SA (1)   Dudley Nourse, SA (9)

Nawab of Pataudi, England (1)   Nawab of Pataudi, Jr, India (6)

Ken Rutherford, NZ (3)   Hamish Rutherford, NZ (1*)

(Number of centuries in brackets; * indicates to date)

IT'S A FACT!

Known for his defensive batting, the former England captain J. W. H. T. Douglas was nicknamed 'Johnny Won't Hit Today' by Australian spectators. An Olympic gold medallist at boxing, he drowned in 1930 trying to save his father following a collision at sea.

BANDS OF BROTHERS

There are many instances of brothers playing first-class cricket, but occasionally the fraternal aggregate has risen above the norm.

THE FOSTERS

In the early years of the twentieth century seven Foster brothers played for Worcestershire, though only four turned out for the county (nicknamed 'Fostershire') at any one time. All seven were primarily batsmen, and three of them went on to captain the side. Harry, the oldest brother, recorded the first double century in the county's first-class history. But the outstanding member of the brotherhood was R. E. 'Tip' Foster, who played eight times for England and scored 287 on his Test debut against Australia in 1903. The score remains the highest by an Englishman in Australia and by any Test debutant. He is also the only player to have captained England at both cricket and football. Tip Foster's remarkable sporting career was cut short by his death at the early age of 36, making him the first of the brothers to die.

THE MOHAMMADS

Four of the Mohammad quintet played Test cricket for Pakistan, and the fifth brother, Raees, was once 12th man. Their combined Test careers spanned 30 years, Wazir and Hanif making their debuts during Pakistan's inaugural series (against India) in 1952–53, Mushtaq following in 1959, Sadiq ten years later. Wazir, the eldest brother, was a dependable batsman in the middle order. Mushtaq, a world-class all-rounder who was at Northamptonshire for several seasons, was an attacking batsman and masterly leg-break bowler. The stylish Sadiq opened the innings for Pakistan and, for some years, for Gloucestershire.

They called Hanif Mohammad 'The Little Master' (until the soubriquet was bestowed on Sachin Tendulkar). He was 17 when he entered the Test arena, already a complete opening batsman with a well-organised defence and phenomenal powers of concentration. He specialised in long innings, his 337 against the West Indies in 1957–58 keeping him at the crease for 16 hours 10 minutes. A year later, playing for Karachi against Bahawalpur, he was run out with his score on 499 off the penultimate ball of the day. He had chanced an extra run fearing that his captain (and sibling) Wazir would declare at their overnight total.

THE HADLEES

The Hadlee brothers – Barry, Dayle and Richard – came from good Kiwi cricketing stock. Their father Walter had toured England either side of the war, captaining the 1949 team. Barry's international career was limited to two ODIs, though he played for Canterbury Province for almost 20 years. Dayle, the second of the trio, won 26 Test caps as a fast-medium bowler, but persistent back trouble eventually forced his retirement from the game.

Richard followed his brother into the New Zealand side in 1973, developing into one of the greatest fast bowlers of all time and one of the finest all-rounders of his era. He was the first bowler to take 400 Test wickets, with perhaps his greatest performance coming at Wellington in 1978, when his match figures of 10 for 100 (6 for 26 in the second innings) earned New Zealand its first ever victory over England. In his final Test appearance, at Edgbaston in 1990, he wrapped up England's second innings with 5 for 53 – by which time he was Sir Richard Hadlee.

THE CHAPPELLS

The Chappell brothers played their cricket hard. Both Ian and Greg captained Australia and scored 36 Test hundreds between them, often batting together. Trevor, the youngest, grew up in their shadow and suffered by comparison. He won only three Test caps but played 20 ODIs. Their grandfather Victor Richardson was an outstanding Australian batsman in the 1930s.

Ian made his Test debut in 1964 and succeeded to the captaincy seven years later, his abrasive leadership taking Australia into a new winning era. Greg took over the reins from his brother in 1975–76, thrashing the West Indies 5–1 in his first series in charge and scoring 702 runs in the process. Less charismatic than his brother, however, he proved to be an efficient rather than inspiring captain. They liked batting together. Against New Zealand at Wellington in 1974, both Chappells scored a century in each innings, a fraternal feat that remains unequalled.

THE EDRICHES

The Edrich clan hailed from Norfolk, and at one period, just after the Second World War, there were four of them on the English county scene. The best known was Bill (W. J.), who had played for England before the war and, along with his regular batting partner Denis Compton, was one of the famous 'Middlesex Twins'. After retiring from Middlesex, the five-times-married

Edrich played Minor Counties cricket for his beloved Norfolk until he was 56.

The oldest of the four and the one with the shortest first-class career, Eric (E. H.) was a batsman of modest achievement who played for Lancashire either side of the hostilities. He was joined at the 'Red Rose' county by Geoff (G. A.), who made a much better fist of things, scoring 26 centuries in his 12 years at Old Trafford and finishing with a respectable batting average of 34.82. Brian (B. R.) was a very useful all-rounder (left-hand bat, right-arm off-breaks), first with Kent, then with Glamorgan. The Surrey and England opener John Edrich was a cousin.

IT'S A FACT!

Alastair Cook, Simon Jones and Marcus Trescothick are among a select group of Test cricketers born on Christmas Day.

SEEING DOUBLE

There have been a number of cricketing twins of both sexes.

ALEC AND ERIC BEDSER

The Surrey pair were confusingly alike, so much so that even teammates sometimes had difficulty telling them apart – except, that is, on the field. As one of the finest ever medium-fast bowlers, Alec towered over his contemporaries; during the eight years he spearheaded the England attack (1946–54), he shared the new ball with no fewer than 14 others. Eric, an off-spinning all-rounder and invaluable member of the county side during its Championship-winning era, never won a Test cap. Having Jim Laker as a fellow off-spinner at Surrey didn't improve his chances!

The story goes that very early on in their careers Alec and Eric tossed a coin to decide which of the two should remain a pace bowler. Eric lost and turned to spin. But for that, England might well have had the good fortune of a Bedser at each end.

MISTAKEN IDENTITY

In June 1981, many sports followers were shocked to learn that the cricketer Alec Bedser had been killed in a car accident in Transvaal. It soon became clear, however, that it was not the great Surrey and England bowler who had died but a South African namesake. Alec and Eric Bedser, born in East London, Cape Province, in 1948, were named after the famous Surrey twins. Both grew up to become more than competent cricketers. Alec, right-hand bat and medium-pace bowler, played three times for Border in the Currie Cup, and Eric was a consistent performer at senior club level.

CECELIA AND ISOBEL JOYCE

Less well known in cricketing circles than their brother Ed (Middlesex, Sussex, England and Ireland), the twin sisters have been regular members of Ireland's women's team for over 15 years. Between them they have clocked up nearly 200 ODI and Twenty20 appearances for their country.

HAMISH AND JAMES MARSHALL

The New Zealand pair have a lot in common beside their genetic connection. Both are batsmen, both have represented their country at Test level and in ODIs (sometimes playing together) and both have fallen short of early expectations. Hamish played in 13 Tests and 66 ODIs before turning his back on international cricket and throwing in his lot with Gloucestershire, where he has had considerable, if not always consistent, success. James, who prefers to open the innings, played fewer Tests and ODIs than his brother and elected to pursue his career on home soil with Northern Districts.

CRAIG AND JAMIE OVERTON

Born in Devon in 1994 (Craig is older by 3 minutes), the Overton twins play for the adjacent county of Somerset. As fast-bowling all-rounders there is little to tell them apart. Jamie is perhaps a shade quicker than his brother, though a little less accurate; Craig bats a place or two higher in the lower order. Assuming they continue to develop and remain free of serious injury, both seem destined to gain international honours – though Craig will have to persuade the selectors, following his two-match ban in 2015, that he can behave himself on the field.

FERNIE AND IRENE SHEVILL

The Australian sisters were the first twins to play Test cricket, though they narrowly missed out on taking to the field together.

Fernie (under her married name Blade) opened the bowling for Australia in the inaugural Test against England at Brisbane in 1934–35. Her sister Rene kept wicket in the second and third matches of the series. That was the beginning and end of the sisters' Test careers, but they made it into the record books.

LIZ AND ROSE SIGNAL

At Headingley in 1984, New Zealand's Signal sisters became the first twins (of either sex) to play Test cricket at the same time. Both were making their debut. Rose batted twice, scoring zero and eight not out; Liz's solitary innings amounted to one. They each bowled nine overs but failed to take a wicket. It would be Rose's only experience of Test cricket; Liz would play five more with little success. It was, nevertheless, a signal honour.

DEREK AND MIKE TAYLOR

For some 15 years, starting in the mid-1960s, the Taylor twins were familiar faces in county cricket. Both were handy performers, playing over 300 matches for their respective counties. Derek (Somerset and Surrey) was a proficient wicketkeeper and more-than-useful batsman, registering a high score of 179. Mike (Nottinghamshire and Hampshire) was a medium-paced all-rounder with over 8,000 runs and 800 wickets to his credit.

STEVE AND MARK WAUGH

The Waugh twins were a cricketing phenomenon. In Test matches they scored 18,956 runs between them, including 52 centuries. In ODIs, the combined total was 16,069 runs with 21 centuries. In addition, Steve captained Australia in 57 Tests (41 of them to victory) and 106 ODIs, winning the 1999 World Cup in the process.

Steve was the first to wear the Baggy Green, making his debut against India at the age of 20. Six years later he was dropped in favour of his brother but swiftly regained his place, and thereafter the twin run machine went into top gear. Their batting styles were different: Steve, all grit and determination; Mark, a sublimely elegant strokemaker. Either way, it was the runs that counted. How relieved the rest of the cricketing world must have been that Mrs Waugh didn't give birth to triplets.

FAMOUS DUOS

● ●

❝ *Man, I am going to miss him terribly.* **❞**
CURTLY AMBROSE (AT THE END OF HIS PLAYING DAYS WITH COURTNEY WALSH)

Many of the best cricketers have prospered in pairs, their coupled names rolling off the tongue as familiarly as Morecambe and Wise: Greenidge and Haynes, Hayden and Langer, Strauss and Cook, among modern openers; fast-bowling duos like Lindwall and Miller, Tyson and Statham, Anderson and Broad. Spinners, for the most part, are more solitary predators. Laker and Lock wreaked havoc for Surrey on the county circuit in the 1950s, though they combined less successfully for England.

Here are some of the game's greatest double acts.

HOBBS AND SUTCLIFFE

Jack Hobbs and Herbert Sutcliffe were, until Andrew Strauss and Alastair Cook overtook their record in 2010, the most prolific openers in Test history. What's more, they reached their total of 3,249 runs in less than half the number of innings it took the new record holders, with an average opening stand of 87.81.

Both batsmen had other regular partners. Hobbs, older by 12 years, opened for Surrey and England before the First World War with Tom Hayward, an early mentor. In 1907, they shared in four three-figure stands during the course of one week. Later, Hobbs regularly opened for England with Yorkshire's Wilfred Rhodes (who had made it all the way up from 11th in the batting order), on one occasion the pair putting on 323 against Australia at Melbourne. Meanwhile, back at the Oval, Andy Sandham (the first batsman to score a Test triple century) had taken over as Hobbs's long-term county partner.

Sutcliffe's own regular opening partner at Yorkshire was Percy Holmes. Against Essex, at Leyton in 1932, the two of them put on 555 for the first wicket, for 45 years a world record. On ten other occasions they shared stands of 250 or more. But it was his seven-year Test partnership with Hobbs that captivated the cricketing public and turned the pair into household names.

Hobbs and Sutcliffe opened for England 38 times. Their first joint appearance in a Test was at Edgbaston against South Africa in 1924. Hobbs was aged 42, Sutcliffe 30. Together they put on 136 runs, the first of 15 opening stands of over 100. They carried on in Australia that winter, with partnerships of 157, 110 and 283 in successive Test innings. In the Melbourne Test they batted throughout the third day – the first such instance in a Test match. Sutcliffe became the first batsman to make a hundred in each innings of a Test against Australia and the first Englishman to score three successive Test centuries. Eighteen months later Hobbs became the first batsman to pass 4,000 runs in Test cricket.

Between them, this remarkable duo notched 348 first-class centuries: Hobbs 199, Sutcliffe 149. Hobbs, who scored his last Test hundred at the age of 46 (still a record), was dubbed 'The Master'. But Herbert Sutcliffe wasn't far behind.

EDRICH AND COMPTON

'The Middlesex Twins' (usually three and four in the batting order) brought much-needed excitement and entertainment to austerity-ridden post-war Britain. Bill Edrich, who had won the Distinguished Flying Cross as a squadron leader in the RAF Bomber Command, was a short, pugnacious batsman who would hook the fiercest bowling from in front of his nose. Denis Compton personified glamour, combining carefree good looks (his normally unruly hair slicked down with Brylcreem in a long-running advertising campaign) with an engagingly cavalier approach to the game that made light of his brilliant batting technique. Both could bowl: Edrich explosively and often erratically fast, Compton with a left-arm unorthodox spin. But it was their spectacular deeds with the bat that caught the eye – and, almost invariably, the opposition bowling attack.

Both had made England debuts before the war, but it was after the cessation of hostilities that they really came into their own. Nineteen forty-seven was their *annus mirabilis*. Compton headed the national batting averages with 3,816 runs at 90.85. Edrich came next with 3,539 runs at 80.43. Compton scored a record 18 centuries, Edrich 12. South Africa was the touring side that year, competing in a five-Test series. This time Edrich topped the averages with 552 runs (110.40) and a highest innings of 191.

Compton totalled 753 runs (94.12) with a top score of 208. It was a long, hot summer, not least for fielding sides when Edrich and Compton were at the crease.

The Middlesex pair continued to clock up plenty of runs for their county and country in the following years but never again reached the zenith of 1947. Compton, who played football for Arsenal and for England in 14 wartime internationals, was increasingly troubled by a recurring knee injury which eventually shortened his career, but not before he and his batting partner had one more claim to glory. At the Oval in 1953, England regained the Ashes after 18 years and 362 days. In front of a delirious crowd, Compton hit the winning runs off part-time bowler Arthur Morris. Backing up at the other end was Bill Edrich.

RAMADHIN AND VALENTINE

In 1950, the West Indies visited England for the first time in 11 years. There were several new faces in the squad, including two young spinners, Sonny Ramadhin (21) and Alf Valentine (20). Both were surprise selections in a side that had a strong batting line-up but was underpowered in the pace department. Little was known about either bowler, since they had played only two first-class matches apiece (the pre-selection trial games) before making the tour.

Ramadhin, the first East Indian to represent the West Indies, was a short, neat figure who wore his sleeves buttoned at the wrist and often bowled wearing a cap. He bowled right-arm off-breaks and leg-breaks with no discernible change of action, using his fingers rather than his wrist to spin the ball. The taller Valentine bowled a left-arm spin of immaculate length, vigorously tweaking the ball to achieve maximum turn. Halfway through the tour it was discovered that he couldn't read the scoreboard from the wicket and was prescribed a pair of NHS glasses, which he wore thereafter.

England comfortably won the first Test at Old Trafford, though Valentine's 8 for 104 in the first innings (11 wickets in the match) was a sign of things to come. And they weren't long coming. The next match at Lord's made cricket history, the West Indies achieving their first ever Test victory in England by a whopping 326 runs. The home side (with the honourable exception of Cyril Washbrook, who made a second-innings hundred) had few answers to the perplexing spin of Ramadhin and Valentine, who took 18 wickets between them. It inspired Egbert Moore (better known as 'Lord Beginner') to write his famous 'Victory Calypso', with its chorus rhythmically commemorating the spinning duo. And soon there was more to celebrate, with the West Indies going on to win the next two Tests and the series 3–1. Valentine finished with 33 wickets (20.42) in the rubber, Ramadhin with 26 (23.23). An otherwise feeble attack resulted in each of them bowling more than a 1,000 overs during the tour.

Seven years later England exacted a cruel revenge. In the first Test at Edgbaston, after Ramadhin (7 for 49 and without his spinning partner) had bowled the West Indies into a strong position, a record second-innings stand of 411 between Peter May (285 not out) and Colin Cowdrey (154) finally turned the tables. But nobody wrote a calypso about them!

NEVER SATISFIED

History began to be made on Christmas Day 1928 in the match between Victoria and New South Wales at Melbourne. In reply to the home side's first innings total of 376, the visitors were 113 for 9 and facing the follow-on. Hal Hooker, New South Wales's last man in, joined his captain Alan Kippax at the crease. The lanky and long-jawed Hooker and the studiously neat and stylish Kippax, one of Australia's leading batsman, made a contrasting pair. They stayed together for 304 minutes, creating a world-record partnership of 307 for the last wicket. Hooker was finally dismissed for 62 (his highest ever score) with the New South Wales total at 420, leaving Kippax stranded on 260 not out. The batsmen received a standing ovation, but for Hooker the enduring memory was of Kippax running down the pitch after his partner's dismissal, shouting, 'You fool! You threw it away! Why didn't you get a hundred?'

LILLEE AND MARSH

Dennis Lillee's name is more often than not coupled with that of Jeff Thomson. They were the most feared bowling combination of the 1970s, destroying first England then the West Indies with their blistering attack. But Lillee's partnership with Australian wicketkeeper Rodney Marsh was no less decisive and even more enduring. Together they made 'Caught Marsh, bowled Lillee' the best-known catchphrase in the game, clocking up a record 95 such dismissals in Test cricket alone.

Both had a belligerent approach on the field. Lillee never concealed his dislike (bordering on contempt) for batsmen, his aggression often spilling over into verbal abuse. But great bowling actions speak louder than words, and in his prime Lillee's positively roared. His bouncer was full of venom and his deadly outswinger fed a constant stream of catches to the predatory Marsh and the slip cordon alongside him. As time went on he sacrificed some of his speed for line and length and movement off the pitch, becoming an even more prolific wicket-taker in the process.

Rodney Marsh's first Test appearance might well have been his last. Chosen more for his batting than his wicketkeeping skills, he was jeeringly dubbed 'Irongloves' by the crowd because of his fumbling of the ball. But, like many a cricketer before him who had made an unpromising start to a Test career, Marsh overcame this initial setback by working at his technique. The selectors wisely persevered with the burly, pugnacious Western Australian, and before long he had become one of the most influential members of the team. He was behind the stumps for practically every ball that Lillee bowled in Test cricket, spectacularly pulling off catch after catch at full stretch.

It was fitting that both men should bow out of Test cricket at the same time – in January 1984, in the fifth Test against Pakistan at Sydney. In one of those statistical quirks with which the history of cricket abounds, both finished with exactly the same record number of dismissals: 355. Typically, Lillee had the last word, taking a wicket with his final ball.

AKRAM AND YOUNIS

Not every great partnership is harmoniously forged. The acrimonious spats between Wasim Akram and Waqar Younis further disrupted an already volatile Pakistan dressing room. According to some of their teammates, the two men were often on non-speaking terms, even on the field, with Inzamam-ul-Haq and others acting as go-betweens. Yet, they combined to create one of the most destructive bowling attacks in the modern game, competitively egged on by each other's success.

Wasim, one of the best left-arm fast bowlers the game has ever seen, was a master of swing and seam, backed up when required by a deadly bouncer or a skilfully concealed slow delivery. He made his Test debut against New Zealand in 1985 and by the time he had finished 17 years later, his tally of Test wickets stood at 414, to which can be added his 502 ODI scalps. As a batsman, given his unquestionable talent, he might be said to have underdelivered, despite a monumental knock of 257 not out against Zimbabwe in 1996.

Waqar joined his fellow Punjabi in the Pakistan side four years later, taking four wickets in India's first innings, including that of another debutant, Sachin Tendulkar, whom he clean bowled for 15. Despite his scorching pace, the climax of a surging approach to the wicket, Waqar rarely resorted to short-pitched bowling. His stock delivery was fast and full, with a lethal late inswing designed to hit the base of the stumps or the batsman's toes, sometimes managing to strike both. Even more damagingly, he perfected the technique of reverse swing. His international span was in tandem with Wasim's, though he played fewer matches overall due to injury. His wicket tally was nevertheless impressive: 373 Test dismissals, 416 in ODIs.

Wasim and Waqar troubled the very best batsmen around the world. When the two of them were on song (even if they weren't singing from the same song sheet) there was no relief to be found at either end. Statistically, they were neck and neck. Wasim took five wickets in a Test innings on 25 occasions; Waqar achieved the feat 22 times. Both registered seven-wicket hauls as their best Test performance. So much in common, yet so little common ground.

IT'S A FACT!

When Ian Botham made his Test debut in 1977, one of his new teammates was Geoffrey Boycott. At the time of Boycott's own debut in 1964, Botham was eight years old.

AMBROSE AND WALSH

In their 49 Tests together Curtly Ambrose and Courtney Walsh took 421 wickets. What can't be quantified is the stress levels afflicted on the batsmen who faced them, for there was no more fearsome aspect in modern cricket than the sight of the two West Indian quickies steaming up to the wicket.

The 6 ft 5 in. (2 m)-tall Antiguan Curtly Ambrose had an inauspicious start to his Test career, his two wickets in the match against Pakistan at Georgetown in 1988 costing 121 runs. But success soon followed, and for the next 12 years Ambrose spearheaded the West Indian attack. No batsman was immune to his extreme pace and lethal bounce. Against Australia at Perth in 1992–93, he took 7 for 25 (7 for 1 in one spell) in the first innings, demolishing a batting line-up that included Justin Langer, David Boon, Alan Border and the two Waughs. A year later it was England's turn, his 6 for 24 in the Trinidad Test helping to skittle out the visitors for a paltry 46. To his final count of 405 wickets in 98 Tests can be added his 225 ODI scalps. Not bad for a man who had really wanted to play baseball!

No fast bowler has ever lasted as long as the Jamaican Courtney Walsh, his Test career stretching to an incredible 17 years. He bowled over 30,000 deliveries (8,000 more than Ambrose) in Test cricket alone, often in much longer spells than pace men are used to. Among fast bowlers, only Glenn McGrath has exceeded his tally of 519 Test wickets, and he was the first to pass 500. He achieved his best Test figures against New Zealand at Wellington in 1994–95: 7 for 37 in the first innings, followed by 6 for 18 in the second. In an ODI match against Sri Lanka in 1986–87, Walsh took 5 for 1, coming on as the fifth bowler. He finished up with 227 ODI wickets, just two more than his partner in pace. There is one record Courtney Walsh has all to himself: an all-time high of 43 ducks in Test cricket. He was lucky he didn't have to face Curtly Ambrose.

JAYAWARDENE AND SANGAKKARA

Partners in spirit, not just at the crease, Mahela Jayawardene and Kumar Sangakkara were the dominant force in Sri Lanka's batting line-up for 15 years. They were never happier than when batting together, which they did a total of 293 times in international cricket. They put on more runs for the third wicket than any other pairing in Test cricket. Against South Africa in the first Test at Colombo in 2006, they came together when the score was 14 for 2 and stayed together for another 624 runs – the highest ever partnership in first-class cricket. Jayawardene's contribution was 374, Sangakkara's a modest 287. The opposition bowling attack included Dale Steyn and Makhaya Ntini, but the runs just kept coming.

Jayawardene made his Test debut at the age of 20. He played in 149 Tests and scored 11,814 runs, his average a shade under 50. His 448 ODI appearances yielded a further 12,650 runs. There was nothing belligerent about his batting; it was all grace and style and studied calm. Statistics show he was less successful outside the subcontinent, where he averaged under 35 compared to over 60 at home. But it was a distinction not always clear to bowlers.

When he retired from international cricket, Sangakkara left a trail of records behind him. He was the first batsman to score innings of over 150 in four consecutive Tests; his 14 scores of over 190 is another Test record. He was the fastest to 8,000, 9,000, 10,000, 11,000 and 12,000 Test runs. His final tally of 12,400 (average 57.40) is the most runs by any left-hander. As a wicketkeeper in ODIs, his 501 dismissals (itself a record) includes a record 99 stumpings. He played in 404 ODIs in all, accumulating another 14,234 runs.

Both men had spells as Sri Lanka's captain. Jayawardene would generally stand at slip, close to his best friend 'Sanga' behind the stumps. Together and separately, the two men have been wonderful ambassadors for the game, their sporting prowess on the field matched by their dignified conduct off it.

IT'S A FACT!

Australia's Bill Lawry and Bobby Simpson are the only opening pair to have scored double centuries in the same Test innings. It happened against the West Indies at Bridgetown in 1964–65, with Lawry making 210, Simpson 201. Together they put on 382 for the first wicket.

IT'S A SCANDAL!

> **❝** *Cricket is unalloyed by love of lucre and mean jealousies.* **❞**
> **LORD FREDERICK BEAUCLERK (1773–1850), FORMER MCC PRESIDENT**

Cricket has had its share of scandals, both on and off the field – from the notorious bodyline Tests in Australia, the fallout from which was felt for more than a decade, to modern-day match-fixing; from players' sexual dalliances to illegal drug-taking; from ball-tampering to fraud. Cricketers have been jailed for a variety of misdemeanours, not all of them cricket related but often tarnishing the image of the sport. Some scandals have been soon forgotten or forgiven. Others have left a more lasting legacy.

DUMPING DOLLY

It had been the elephant in the room for some time. Now, with the 1968–69 tour of South Africa imminent, the question of whether Basil D'Oliveira would be selected for the team became a hot topic. D'Oliveira, a 'Cape Coloured' barred from playing first-class cricket in his own country on racial grounds, had come to England in 1960 to continue his career. Six years later he made his Test debut for England and had been a regular member of the side ever since. Anticipating problems, envoys from the MCC, who in those days selected England touring parties, visited South Africa to discuss the matter, among them the former prime minister Sir Alec Douglas-Home. It was made clear by the South African government that D'Oliveira's inclusion in the side would not be acceptable.

The Worcestershire all-rounder had been in and out of the England side during the 1968 series against Australia, but returning for the final Test at the Oval he scored an impressive 158 in the first innings. However, when the 16-man touring party was announced five days later, D'Oliveira's name was missing. The all-rounder berth was filled by Tom Cartwright of Warwickshire. The public response to the news was mixed. Some supported the decision, pointing to D'Oliveira's age (37) and his uncertain form of the summer. Others, including some of its own membership, accused the MCC of sympathising with the South African apartheid regime, though in truth it was more a case of maintaining sporting links at all costs. The British minister for sport, Denis Howell, sought assurances that the selection had been made on cricketing grounds alone.

Matters came to a head on 16 September when Tom Cartwright withdrew from the side through injury. D'Oliveira was immediately named as his replacement. An angry John Vorster, South Africa's prime minister, accused the MCC and others of being politically motivated, saying, 'Guests who have ulterior motives usually find they are not invited.' A week later, the beleaguered cricket authority reluctantly called off the tour and South Africa's sporting isolation began. As for the man at the centre of the storm, he continued to play Test cricket for England for another four years.

CLOSE ENCOUNTER

Two of the most abrasive players of the modern era, Dennis Lillee and Javed Miandad, were involved in an ugly confrontation at Perth in 1981 during the first Test against Pakistan. Lillee appeared to impede the Pakistan captain as he was going for a run, then aimed a kick at him. Miandad retaliated by threatening to strike Lillee with his bat. Before the two men could come to blows, umpire Tony Crafter stepped in and separated them as if in a boxing ring. Most observers blamed Lillee for the incident, though Miandad was hardly faultless. The Australian received a derisory $120 fine and a two-match ban (minor ODIs). Miandad got off scot-free.

DIRTY HANDS

The first Test between England and South Africa at Lord's in July 1994 was a landmark event – the first such meeting between the two countries for 29 years, South Africa's long period of banishment from international cricket at last behind them. In front of a full house the visitors began well, posting a first innings total of 357 (105 from skipper Kepler Wessels) before dismissing England for 180. By the afternoon of the third day, South Africa, batting again, had built up a substantial lead.

It was at this point, just before the tea interval, that the drama began. Live television footage showed England's captain, the 25-year-old Mike Atherton, seemingly tampering with the ball by rubbing it with dirt taken from his pocket. Atherton's later explanation to the England management team of Ray Illingworth and Keith Fletcher was that he had been merely maintaining (as opposed to illegally changing) the condition of the ball by absorbing the sweat on it. However, when hauled before the match referee, the former bellicose Australian batsman Peter Burge, Atherton claimed he was doing nothing more than drying his hands. It was a confused and clumsy defence. At a hastily convened press conference Illingworth announced that the England captain was being fined £2,000 (half for the dirty deed itself, half for not coming clean with the match referee), though Burge said later that he would have favoured a stiffer two-match suspension. South Africa went on to win the Test by 356 runs, despatching the home side for a humiliating 99 in their second innings.

In the furore that followed there were widespread calls for the England captain to be sacked, but the selectors kept their heads and Atherton his job, and a defiant knock of 99 in the next Test aided his redemption. But there was a postscript to the scandal. When, in the third and final Test, Atherton was dismissed first ball (LBW to pace bowler Fanie de Villiers), he was seen to shake his head in disappointment as he left the field. An unforgiving Peter Burge, officiating once again, chose to construe the gesture as dissent and fined Atherton 50 per cent of his match fee.

IT'S A FACT!

....

Sir Alec Douglas-Home is the only British prime minister to have played first-class cricket. As Lord Dunglass (his title at the time) he played ten first-class matches in the 1920s for Oxford University, Middlesex and the MCC. As befits a politician, he was an all-rounder.

CAPTAIN CORRUPT

If one man seemed to embody cricket's finest values, it was the clean-cut, personable South African captain Wessel Johannes 'Hansie' Cronje – that is, until 7 April 2000, when Delhi police charged him with 'fixing' the outcome of South Africa's ODIs against India the previous month. The police released a transcript of an alleged conversation between Cronje and an Indian bookmaker named Sanjay Chawla, which also implicated three other players – Herschelle Gibbs, Nicky Boje and Pieter Strydom. Cronje initially denied the allegations but four days later confessed to the South African Cricket Board's chief executive, Ali Bacher, that he had indeed received sums of $10,000–$15,000 for information about team selection, though he had not, he stressed, been involved in match-fixing.

Cronje, a veteran of 68 Tests and 188 ODIs (53 and 138 as captain), was promptly sacked. A commission of enquiry was set up in June under Judge Edwin King. The cricket world looked on in disbelief as the disgraced skipper's teammates reluctantly gave evidence, one shocking revelation following another. Gibbs and seam bowler Henry Williams both testified that Cronje had offered them $15,000 apiece to underperform in an ODI – though in the event neither had followed through on the deal. All-rounder Strydom stated that Cronje had approached him on similar grounds before one of the Test matches against India. The court made an offer of its own to Cronje: immunity from criminal prosecution in exchange for full disclosure. South African cricket's hitherto exemplary figurehead named other names (including that of his Indian opposite number, Mohammad Azharuddin), broke down in tears and confessed that he had an 'unfortunate love of money'.

The International Cricket Council (ICC) launched an investigation into what was now believed to be widespread corruption in the sport, especially on the subcontinent, which led to further convictions. Herschelle Gibbs and Henry Williams were banned from international cricket for six months. Cronje's banishment was for life and extended to every level of the game. Two years later, he was killed when the small plane in which he was travelling crashed in the country's Western Cape province. Many South Africans, still in denial over their erstwhile sporting hero's corrupt past, took the opportunity to elevate him to cult status.

IT'S A FACT!

Master Soviet spy Kim Philby lived out his final years in Moscow. Despite his unsporting profession, he remained a keen cricket fan and kept abreast of the game by reading back issues of *The Times*.

DODGY SAMPLE

The 2003 World Cup, jointly hosted by South Africa, Zimbabwe and Kenya, had barely got underway when the Australian Cricket Board made the shock announcement that a drugs sample from the leg-spinner Shane Warne had proved positive and that they were referring the matter to the Anti-Doping Policy Committee. The random sample had been taken in Sydney on 22 January, some three weeks before, and revealed traces of a prescription drug called Moduretic, routinely used in the treatment of hypertension, high blood pressure and fluid retention. Though the diuretic itself was not a performance enhancing drug, it was prohibited on the grounds that it could be used as a masking agent for steroids.

It was no secret that Warne had been undergoing an intensive fitness programme in recent months following a dislocated shoulder. Losing weight had been a key objective. At a hurriedly convened press conference before flying back to Australia for further tests, the bowler said he was 'shocked and absolutely devastated' by the revelations, though he did admit to taking a fluid tablet. In a subsequent statement to the media, Warne claimed that it was his mother who had given him the now notorious pill to help him shed a few pounds. He added, 'I have never taken performance-enhancing drugs, and I do not condone their use.' Ten days later, the results of a second sample having confirmed those of the first, Australia's star leg-spinner was banned by the Australian Cricket Board from all forms of cricket for a period of one year. It could have been worse; the standard suspension was for two years, but since there was no direct evidence of steroid use the bowler was treated leniently.

The 33-year-old Warne insisted that he was a victim of anti-doping hysteria, though public opinion seemed to support the punishment meted out. There was widespread speculation that his international career was now at an end. But that was to underestimate one of cricket's most enduring characters. A couple of weeks after the ban's expiry date, Warne was named in the Australian squad for the upcoming tour of Sri Lanka.

POLITICAL PROTEST

During the World Cup match against Namibia at Harare in 2003, Zimbabwean players Andy Flower and Henry Olonga took to the field wearing black armbands. They were protesting against President Robert Mugabe's regime and what they described as the 'death of democracy' in their country. This courageous gesture led to government accusations of treason, a crime that carries the death penalty in Zimbabwe. Faced with the prospect of a prison sentence at the very least, both men cut short their international careers after the tournament and fled the country. Flower later became the England coach, while Olonga moved into the commentary box.

FOOL'S GOLD

When the Texan billionaire Allen Stanford rode into town (actually it was Lord's and he arrived by helicopter) in June 2008, dollar signs started flashing in the corporate eyes of the England and Wales Cricket Board (ECB). During a televised presentation at the sport's headquarters, with cricketing knights Sir Ian Botham and Sir Viv Richards acting as co-hosts, the ECB announced that it had struck a lucrative deal with the US financier. England would play a series of five Twenty20 matches in the Caribbean against a Stanford Superstars XI. Up for grabs was a winner-takes-all $20-million pot for each game.

Stanford, a dual citizen of the USA and the twin-island nation of Antigua and Barbuda, already funded a West Indian Twenty20 tournament which bore his name, and had built his own ground in Antigua. Five months after the deal with the ECB was signed, his Superstars took to the field (his field) against a much-touted England XI and promptly thrashed them by ten wickets, earning themselves close to $1 million a head. The superstar leading the charge was none other than Chris Gayle, with an undefeated 65 off 45 balls. Televised pictures of Stanford being overfamiliar with some of the England players' wives and girlfriends while their partners struggled to stem the flow of West Indian runs added to the post-match gloom in the visitors' dressing room.

It was the only one of the scheduled matches to be played. In February 2009, the US Securities and Exchange Commission charged Stanford with fraud and multiple violations of US financial regulations, including a $7 billion Ponzi scheme. An embarrassed ECB swiftly severed its connections with their benefactor of the year before. The knighthood bestowed on Stanford by a grateful Antigua and Barbuda in 2006 was rescinded three years later. Sentenced to 110 years in jail, the Texas money man has vowed to clear his name. He has plenty of time in which to do it.

SLEDGING

The term 'sledging' is used to describe the practice of undermining a batsman's concentration by making distracting remarks while he is at the crease. The word was coined in Australia in the mid-1960s, though its precise origin is unknown. One popular theory is that when a certain batsman arrived at the wicket, it being known that he was having an affair with a teammate's wife, the opposition fielders chorused the old Percy Sledge number 'When a Man Loves a Woman'.

It was nothing new for batsmen to be on the receiving end of ribald comments, but generally it would be more good-humoured banter than gamesmanship. The tone changed in the 1970s, with Australian teams, in particular, stepping up the verbal abuse. Wicketkeeper Rod Marsh was one of the most vocal, on one occasion saying to England batsman Derek Randall, 'Your mother wanted a girl and your father wanted a boy. But they had you, so they were both happy.'

Bowlers joined in too. 'Hospital food suit you?' said Aussie pace man Craig McDermott to England tail-ender Phil Tufnell on a lively pitch at Perth. The moustachioed Merv Hughes would say to any number of England batsmen, 'Does your f****** husband play cricket as well?' or 'If you just turn the bat over, you'll find the instructions on the other side.'

The story goes that when Zimbabwe's last man in, Eddo Brandes, continued to defy Glenn McGrath against all the odds, the exasperated bowler insultingly enquired, 'Eddo, why are you so fat?' The overweight Brandes gave as good as he got, retorting, 'Because every time I make love to your wife, she gives me a biscuit.'

All sides are guilty of sledging, though it might be said that the Australians have almost turned it into an art form. Some comments go beyond the acceptable; some, if they are in Urdu or Afrikaans, pass incomprehensibly over the heads of those to whom they are directed. One thing is sure: we haven't heard the last word.

INJURY TIME

· ·

> ❝ *I'm having a sore back maybe because*
> *I'm swinging the bat so hard.* ❞
> **BRENDON McCULLUM, NEW ZEALAND BATSMAN**

Cricket is often light-heartedly portrayed as a placid, somewhat soporific sport, whose leisurely activity barely intrudes upon its dozing spectators. In reality of course, and especially at the highest level, the contest between bat and ball can be a brutally painful and physically damaging experience. Here are some bruising encounters that left their mark.

CRUNCH TIME

A sickening on-field collision on the second day of the first Test against Sri Lanka at Kandy in 1999 left Australians Steve Waugh and Jason Gillespie with horrific injuries. Both fielders were attempting to catch a top edge from batsman Mahela Jayawardene off the bowling of off-spinner Colin Miller, Waugh running back from short fine leg, Gillespie charging in from deep backward square leg. Watching from the players' balcony, physiotherapist

Errol Alcott anticipated the collision and was on the boundary edge with his emergency medical kit almost before it happened.

It was the Australian captain, Waugh, clutching the bridge of his bloodied and broken nose, who initially received most of the attention. Gillespie, although he remained sitting on the ground, appeared to be in less distress (Tony Greig, on commentary at the time, speculated over the airwaves that 'maybe his knee is buggered'). In fact, it was the pace man's left shin that had been shattered. Neither player, incidentally, had managed to catch the ball. A helicopter landed on the outfield to airlift the injured pair to a hospital in Colombo – an episode that in the words of *Wisden* was 'reminiscent of a scene out of *Apocalypse Now*'. Not one to stay out of the action for long, Steve Waugh, his nose still plastered, returned to lead his side in the second Test. His damaged fast bowler, however, was sidelined for several months.

DENTAL CARE

A snow-affected pitch at Buxton in a county match between Derbyshire and Lancashire in June 1975 had the ball lifting dangerously off a length. Derbyshire batsman Ashley Harvey-Walker handed umpire Dickie Bird something wrapped in a handkerchief. It was his false teeth. The generally jovial Harvey-Walker, sometimes called Ashley Hearty-Whacker because of his strong-arm tactics with the bat, didn't stay long at the crease, being dismissed for just seven. On his way back to the pavilion he collected his teeth from the umpire.

LAST HURRAH

As they walked out to open England's second innings against the West Indies at Old Trafford in 1976, the combined age of Brian Close and John Edrich was 84. There was just 65 minutes' play left on Saturday (the third day) and the home side had been set the small task of scoring 552 to win. Given that they had been blown apart for 71 in the first innings by the West Indian trio of fast bowlers Michael Holding (5 for 17), Andy Roberts (3 for 22) and Wayne Daniel (2 for 13), few gave them much of a chance. All three speed merchants routinely topped 145 kph (90 mph) and the two batsmen knew they were in for a torrid time.

Neither was unused to the painful effects of fast bowling. Edrich had had two ribs broken by Dennis Lillee a couple of years before, and Close had unflinchingly stood up to Wes Hall and Charlie Griffith at their fastest at Lord's in 1963, a match in which Colin Cowdrey had suffered a broken arm. Like two old gunfighters facing a final showdown, the veteran pair (without helmets, arm guards or chest protectors) were subjected to a barrage of viciously targeted, short-pitched bowling. When Edrich asked his partner between overs what he thought was the best way to play it, Close replied, 'With your chest.' And so they did. When they returned to the dressing room at the close of play, their wickets still intact, both sported an array of shocking bruises to prove it. They put on 54 for the first wicket, then watched as England disintegrated once more, all out for 126 (Roberts 6 for 37). Neither player was called upon by his country again.

CLOSE CALL

Australian batsman Graham Yallop was the first player to wear a helmet in a Test match. It was 1978. Sixteen years before, the Indian opener Nari Contractor almost died when struck on the head by a ball from Charlie Griffith in a tour match against Barbados. It took two major operations to save Contractor's life – West Indies captain Frank Worrell being the first to donate blood for a transfusion. Although he eventually returned to first-class cricket (with a steel plate in his skull), Contractor's Test career was knocked on the head.

FAULTY PITCH

Sabina Park, Jamaica, was the venue for the first Test between the West Indies and England in January 1998. England's captain Mike Atherton won the toss and elected to bat, but after 10.1 overs the tourists were 17 for 3, with Atherton, Mark Butcher and Nasser Hussein all back in the pavilion, victims of the West Indian pace duo of Ambrose and Walsh and of the uneven bounce. With the ball lifting dangerously off a length, the England physiotherapist Wayne Morton made six trips onto the field to administer pain-killing spray to arms and fingers.

Mike Atherton finally put a stop to the bruising encounter by summoning Alec Stewart and Graham Thorpe off the field; the two men at the crease had both been struck several times as they tried to fend off the ball. In making his dramatic gesture, the England skipper insisted that the safety of the players was paramount. The match referee, former Australian wicketkeeper Barry Jarman, agreed, and 90 minutes later the game was officially called off – the first time in Test cricket's 122-year history that a dangerous pitch had been cited as the reason for an abandonment.

The two sides reconvened a week later at Port-of-Spain, Trinidad, for a hurriedly arranged additional Test, which the West Indies won by three wickets. As a postscript to the Jamaican game, the ICC ruled that, despite its abandoned status, all performances should count towards career records. A stipulation that, as far as England's batsmen were concerned, added insult to injury.

IT'S A FACT!

In the second Test against Australia at Melbourne in 1968, the West Indian batsman Seymour Nurse was caught at deep fine leg after the ball had rebounded off the (helmetless) head of the fielder at backward short leg.

HEART-STOPPING

After losing the 1974–75 Ashes series 4–1, the England side crossed the Tasman Sea for the New Zealand leg of the tour. In the first Test at Auckland the England batsmen, liberated from the hostilities of Lillee and Thomson, piled up 593 for 6 before declaring. New Zealand replied with 326 and, made to follow on, were 140 for 9 in their second innings when Test debutant Ewen Chatfield walked to the crease.

Although not known for his batting skills, the 24-year-old Chatfield stoically supported the experienced Geoff Howarth at the other end, and the pair were still there at the close of play. The partnership continued when the match resumed on Monday (Sunday being a rest day), obstinately lifting the score to 184. It was then that the Lancashire fast bowler Peter Lever bowled a bouncer at Chatfield, who deflected the ball off his glove into his left temple. He collapsed unconscious onto the ground. There was no doctor on hand, but the veteran England physiotherapist Bernard Thomas ran onto the field.

Chatfield had swallowed his tongue and his heart actually stopped beating for a few seconds. While the players anxiously looked on, with Lever himself distraught, Thomas applied mouth-to-mouth resuscitation and gave the stricken batsman heart massage. Although he didn't regain full consciousness on the field, he was able to be transported to hospital and subsequently made a full recovery – and 42 more Test appearances for New Zealand. No one was more relieved than the blameless Peter Lever.

OUCH! THE FIVE MOST COMMON CRICKET INJURIES

- Hamstring strain
- Lower-back pain
- Side strain
- Shoulder pain
- Sprained ankles

LUCKY BREAK

Along with big Joel Garner, Malcolm Marshall spearheaded the West Indian attack in the series against England in 1984. In the first Test at Edgbaston he cut short Andy Lloyd's all-too-brief Test career with a blow to his helmeted head. In the next match at Lord's he had England's batsmen on the hop once again, picking up a further eight wickets. So it was with barely concealed relief that the England team at Headingley, for the third Test, witnessed Marshall breaking his left thumb in two places while fielding in the gully. Admittedly, it wasn't his bowling arm, but there was little likelihood of him playing much of a role for the rest of the match, or indeed in the one to follow.

In reply to England's first innings total of 270, the West Indies were 290 for 9 when Marshall, his arm in plaster, came out to join Larry Gomes, not out on 96. Marshall batted one-handed long enough for Gomes to reach three figures and the West Indies to 302 all out.

One can imagine the consternation in the England camp when Marshall took to the field for their second innings, even more so when he took the new ball. Bowling 26 hostile overs, his arm still encased, he took the England batting line-up apart, finishing with 7 for 53, his best Test figures to date. Dismissing the home side for 159, the West Indies won the match by eight wickets. A thumbs-up for Malcolm Marshall.

BIG HITTER

On his Test debut for Australia in 1894–95, Albert Trott took 8 for 43 in England's second innings to win the match for his country. But when he was omitted from the side (captained by his brother Harry) to tour England a year later, he left home under his own steam and signed up for Middlesex. Primarily a slow bowler and lusty middle-order batsman, Trott made a huge impact on the English scene. He took all ten wickets in an innings against Somerset in 1900, and seven years later, in a benefit match against the same county, took four wickets in four balls, followed by a hat-trick later in the same innings. With the match wrapped up early, the beneficiary wryly observed that he was 'bowling himself into the workhouse'. He is best remembered, though, for his legendary hit over the pavilion at Lord's in 1899. It happened, fittingly, against the Australians, with Trott playing for the MCC. Since the ball didn't quite go out of the ground (the rules for a six), the historic blow earned him only four runs. Trott, who also played two Tests for England, tragically took his own life in 1914.

SNOWED DOWN UNDER

The 1970–71 Ashes series was the longest rubber in Test history. Six matches were scheduled, but with the third Test having been abandoned without a ball being bowled, a seventh was added. This took place at Sydney with England one up in the series. Australia had just overhauled England's first innings total of 184 with seven wickets down, when a short-pitched delivery from John Snow hit leg-spinner Terry Jenner on the side of the head. The batsman staggered and fell to the ground, clutching his temple.

Snow, England's premier strike bowler, already had form in the series. In the fourth Test another short ball had struck tail-ender Graham McKenzie in the face. Now the Sydney crowd reacted angrily as Jenner was assisted from the field. At the end of the over, when Snow returned to his position on the fine-leg boundary alongside Paddington Hill, a drunken spectator grabbed him by the shirt. Dozens of beer cans were hurled onto the grass. Fellow fast bowler Bob Willis ran to Snow's aid and moved him out of the danger area. The England captain, Ray Illingworth, took his players off the field and refused to return until the debris had been cleared and order restored.

Jenner eventually resumed his innings, but England won the match and regained the Ashes. As for John Snow, he fractured the little finger on his right hand when, in trying to make a catch during Australia's second innings, he collided with the boundary fence. No beer cans were thrown.

FREAK INJURIES

Middlesex and England off-spinner Fred Titmus had four toes sliced off his left foot by a boat's propeller while swimming in the sea during the 1967–68 tour of the West Indies. Amazingly, he was playing cricket eight weeks later.

New Zealand all-rounder Trevor Franklin suffered multiple leg fractures when he was mowed down by a motorised baggage trolley at Gatwick Airport in 1986, keeping him out of the game for 18 months.

The England all-rounder Chris Lewis was dubbed 'The Prat without a Hat' by *The Sun* newspaper after he suffered severe sunstroke during a match against Antigua in 1994, having taken to the field without any protective covering on his shaven head.

In 2006, Australian opener Matthew Hayden was attacked by a dog while jogging near his home and sustained a 5-cm (2-in.) gash on his ankle. At the time he'd been recovering from a broken finger.

When Ted Dexter's car ran out of petrol in West London in 1965, the former England captain decided to push it. He lost control of the vehicle, which rolled back onto him and crushed his leg, cutting short his Test career.

IT'S A FACT!

In 1796, 11 one-armed men played 11 one-legged men in a cricket match in south London. The one-legged XI won by 103 'runnings' and then ran a 100-yard (91-m) race for a prize of 20 guineas.

TEN TIPS FOR PREVENTING INJURIES

- Always warm up before a game or practice session.

- Wear protective gear in the nets as well as when out in the middle.

- Make sure your protective equipment fits securely and is adequate for the task.

- Wear cricket boots that are comfortable and give proper support, with studs that grip on a damp surface.

- Maintain a good level of fitness during the off-season.

- Don't be tempted to play if you are carrying a minor injury; it will simply aggravate it.

- Make sure that there is always a first-aid kit on hand, along with someone experienced in using it.

- Young bowlers, especially, should receive proper coaching advice about their bowling action, to avoid long-term back stress.

- Don't imitate professional cricketers too closely, especially when it comes to diving about in the field; they get paid to take risks.

- Always wear sunscreen, and a cap or sunhat if you are a bit thin on top!

CRICKET MEETS
THE ARTS

> *I suppose doing a love scene with Raquel Welch roughly corresponds to scoring a century before lunch.*
> **OLIVER REED, ACTOR**

There has always been a strong bond between the worlds of cricket and theatre, the on-field drama seemingly resonating with that onstage. The Scottish dramatist J. M. Barrie, creator of Peter Pan, founded his own cricket team, the Allahakbarries. Arthur Conan Doyle, P. G. Wodehouse and A. A. Milne were among the writers who regularly turned out for Barrie's distinctly literary side. Not all of them took these Edwardian escapades on the cricket field seriously, though Conan Doyle was an accomplished club cricketer and once, when playing for the MCC, clean bowled W. G. Grace – but not before the great man had scored 110. This prize wicket was Conan Doyle's only scalp in first-class cricket and prompted him to write a celebratory 19-verse poem on the subject.

P. G. Wodehouse represented his school, Dulwich College, as a medium-fast bowler. Until he took up permanent residency in America, the affable 'Plum' was an enthusiastic follower of the game. He famously named the immortal Jeeves after a Warwickshire cricketer killed at the Battle of the Somme. The Yorkshire-born Percy Jeeves was a promising all-rounder for his adopted county Warwickshire, good enough to be selected for the Gentlemen v Players in 1914 and who but for the war might well have gone on to win an England cap.

IT'S A FACT!

The author Sir Arthur Conan Doyle adapted the names of two contemporary Derbyshire cricketers, Frank Shacklock and Thomas Mycroft, for the characters Sherlock Holmes and his brother Mycroft.

CRICKETING LAUREATE

Another man of the theatre and once a keen cricketer was the Irish avant-garde playwright and novelist Samuel Beckett, author of *Waiting for Godot*. Beckett, who was awarded the Nobel Prize in Literature in 1969, spent most of his adult life in Paris and moved in circles far removed from cricket. Yet the writer never lost his interest in the game, forged when he was a schoolboy in Dublin. A left-hand opening bat and medium-pace bowler, he played two first-class games for

Dublin University against Northamptonshire in the 1920s but with little success (his highest score in four innings was 18 and he failed to take a wicket). It was enough, though, to get a mention in *Wisden* (the first Nobel Laureate to have achieved this distinction), an acknowledgement that both amused and delighted Beckett.

PINTERESQUE

Harold Pinter, who as a playwright was greatly influenced by Samuel Beckett, never played first-class cricket. For many years, however, he was the leading light of the Gaieties Cricket Club (founded in 1937 by the music hall artist Lupino Lane), first as a player, then as captain and finally as chairman. Despite his London East End upbringing, Pinter was a lifetime supporter of Yorkshire County Cricket Club. Cricket metaphors and references abound in his work: two films for which he wrote screenplays – *Accident* and *The Go-Between* – feature cricket matches, but the biggest clue to the writer's lifelong love of the game comes in his play *No Man's Land*. Each of the four characters in the play, referred to by their surnames only, shares the name of a famous English cricketer of the so-called Golden Age: Hirst (George), Spooner (Reginald), Briggs (Johnny) and Foster (Frank of Warwickshire, a fine all-rounder and no relation of the seven Worcestershire Fosters). The dramatic work itself, however, has nothing whatsoever to do with the sport.

PLAYS AND PLAYERS

Several contemporary dramatists have been enthusiastic club cricketers, among them Tom Stoppard, David Hare, Ronald Harwood and Alan Ayckbourn. But none can match the cricketing CV of Peter Gibbs, the Derbyshire batsman turned stage and television playwright, who scored over 10,000 runs for the county, including 11 centuries. His first screenplay, *Arthur's Hallowed Ground*, was about a club groundsman and the sacred turf he had tended for 45 years.

THE FINAL TEST

Terence Rattigan, whose hugely popular plays include *The Browning Version*, *Separate Tables* and *The Deep Blue Sea*, transferred his love of cricket onto the big screen. Rattigan had been a talented schoolboy cricketer, opening the innings for Harrow against Eton in the annual fixture at Lord's in 1929 and scoring a solid 29. His school report at cricket was succinctly expressed: 'He has played many fine innings. His off-side strokes are masterful, especially those behind point. His bowling has lost a lot of the accuracy it had last year. His fielding at slip has been excellent.'

The Final Test began life as a television play before being adapted for the cinema in 1953. Veteran England batsman Sam Palmer (played by Jack Warner) is about to make his last Test appearance, after a long and successful career, against Australia at the Oval. Interwoven with the build-up to this momentous event are a characteristic Rattigan father–son relationship and a romantic subplot. Newsreel footage of England v Australia at the Oval helps create an authentic atmosphere, as do the somewhat self-conscious walk-on roles of Sam Palmer's teammates, the real-life Len Hutton, Denis Compton, Alec Bedser, Jim Laker, Cyril Washbrook and Godfrey Evans.

TEN MOVIES WITH CRICKET IN THE FRAME

It's Not Cricket (1949)
British comedy that involves a pair of inept private eyes and a cricket ball with a stolen diamond inside.

P'tang, Yang, Kipperbang (1982)
Coming-of-age story about a cricket-obsessed schoolboy.

Bodyline (1984)
TV drama about the infamous England tour Down Under in 1932–33.

Playing Away (1987)
Comedy about an English village club that stages a Third World cricket week.

Wondrous Oblivion (2003)
Cricket meets racial bigotry in 1960s London.

Iqbal (2005)
A Bollywood story about a deaf-mute boy who dreams of playing cricket for India.

Hit for Six (2007)
Barbadian drama about match-fixing, featuring several famous West Indian cricketers.

Hansie (2008)
The decline and fall of South Africa's disgraced captain Hansie Cronje.

Fire in Babylon (2010)
Documentary about the all-conquering West Indies side of the 1970s and 1980s.

Howzat! Kerry Packer's War (2010)
Dramatised account of how the Australian media tycoon changed the face of cricket forever.

CRICKET: THE MUSICAL

Having not worked together since the successful launch of their musical *Evita* in 1978, Tim Rice and his collaborator Andrew Lloyd Webber were commissioned by Prince Edward to write a show for the Queen's 60th birthday. A self-confessed cricket addict with his own team, the Heartaches (the club's motto, '*Clava recta*', means 'A straight bat'), Rice leapt at the chance.

The result of their revived partnership was a 25-minute mini-musical entitled *Cricket*, first performed at Windsor Castle on 18 June 1986. Trevor Nunn directed the production, which light-heartedly tells the story of a young cricketer forced to make a choice between the demands of his girlfriend and the requirements of his team. Most of the characters have spoof names that are cricket related: Donald Hobbs, the Earl of Headingley and his daughter Emma Kirkstall-Lane, and a West Indian fast bowler named Winston B. Packer. There is no spoken dialogue and among the show's 11 songs are 'The Summer Game', 'The Art of Bowling', 'The Final Stand' and the concluding number 'One Hot Afternoon'. *Cricket*, graciously received on the night, was staged only twice more and Lloyd Webber went on to use several of the tunes in his later musical *Aspects of Love*.

ALL-STAR XI

The Hollywood Cricket Club was founded in 1932 by the English stage and screen actor Charles Aubrey Smith. Smith's other claim to fame was as a cricketer, having captained England to victory in his only Test match – against South Africa at Port Elizabeth in 1889, the first international encounter between the two countries. Known as 'Round the Corner' Smith because of his oddly curved run-up as a bowler (W. G. Grace once remarked, 'It is rather startling when he suddenly appears at the bowling crease'), he won a cricket blue at Cambridge and went on to play for Sussex for the next 14 years. In his solitary Test appearance he took seven wickets with his right-arm medium pace, including 5 for 19 in South Africa's first innings.

Essentially Sunday cricketers, the Hollywood club took itself seriously enough to have its own predictably flamboyant uniform: a blazer with magenta, mauve and black stripes, and a harlequin-style cap. Errol Flynn (Tasmanian by birth), Laurence Olivier, Boris Karloff (real name William Pratt and a lifetime supporter of Surrey), who kept wicket, David Niven and the Sherlock Holmes/Dr Watson duo of Basil Rathbone and Nigel Bruce were among the expat cricketers of variable talent who turned out for the celebrity team. P. G. Wodehouse was the club's first secretary.

As a subtle nod to his cricketing past, C. Aubrey Smith (as he was known onscreen) named his Beverly Hills home 'The Round Corner'. He was knighted in 1944 for his contribution to Anglo-American friendship.

CRICKETING INSPIRATION

The father of the writer H. G. Wells was the first cricketer to take four wickets in four balls in a first-class match. Joseph Wells, a Kent professional who bowled round-arm at pace, performed the feat for his county against Sussex at Brighton in 1862. His son, whose fame was to outstrip that of his father, always professed to have no interest in cricket. Is it then simply a coincidence that the eponymous hero of one of his most celebrated novels, Kipps, shares the name of a well-known eighteenth-century Kent cricketer?

HOORAY FOR BOLLYWOOD

Cricket and the Indian film industry are inextricably linked, their star performers sharing the adulation of the masses. A number of top Indian cricketers have acted on the big screen – among them Sunil Gavaskar, Sandeep Patel, Ajay Jadeja, Kapil Dev, Syed Kirmani, Vinod Kambli and Yuvraj Singh (whose father Yograj Singh is a well-known actor). Sachin Tendulkar appears as himself (after all, who else could play those shots?) in the biopic *Sachin: A Billion Dreams*.

Bollywood in spirit, though actually shot in Sydney, is the Indo-Australian romantic comedy *UNindian*, with former fast bowler Brett Lee as the male lead. Those (including many anxious batsmen) who watched the former Australian speedster charging up to the wicket may find his change of career unlikely. But beneath the menace, 'Bing', as his teammates called him, was never short on charm.

IT'S A FACT!

During the interval at the ODI between New Zealand and England at Wellington in 2002, film director Peter Jackson conducted 30,000 cricket fans in a series of howling, growling and grunting noises. They were sound effects for a battle scene in *The Two Towers*, part of the *Lord of the Rings* trilogy.

POETS CORNER

Probably the most famous poet to play cricket at Lord's (though it was the original ground, not the present site) was Lord Byron. In 1805, aged 17, he appeared for Harrow in the first of what would become an annual fixture against Eton. Byron scored seven 'notches' in the first innings and two in the second. Because of his club foot he batted with a runner. His experiences of schoolboy cricket were commemorated in his poem 'Cricket at Harrow'.

The First World War poet Siegfried Sassoon was an even keener cricketer, though of modest ability. One of his earliest poems, 'The Extra Inch', published in *Cricket* magazine when Sassoon was a 16-year-old schoolboy at Marlborough College, describes a batsman facing up to his first ball and being bowled 'neck and crop'. The last verse reads:

> Full sad and slow pavilionwards he walked.
> The careless critics talked;
> Some said that he was yorked;
> A half-volley at a pinch.
> The batsman murmured as he inward stalked,
> 'It was the extra inch.'

In later life, when the horrors of the First World War had receded (though they would never disappear), the poet sought solace in sunlit games of cricket played at Heytesbury House, his Wiltshire home, where estate workers rubbed shoulders with the gentry and those who were clean bowled or narrowly missed a catch in the slips knew all about the 'extra inch'.

The poet Alan Ross doubled up for many years as cricket correspondent for *The Observer*. Another commentator on the sport who wrote poetry was John Arlott, one of whose best-known works is a poetic tribute to the great English batsman Sir Jack Hobbs on his 70th birthday in 1952. The most unlikely published poet is the former England fast bowler John Snow, a fearsome prospect with ball in hand but between the lines a man of great sensitivity. He produced two volumes of verse while still playing for England, *Contrasts* (1971) and *Moments and Thoughts* (1973).

'THE SURREY POET'

Albert Craig was born near Huddersfield in 1849 but eventually made his way to London, where he peddled his verses about cricket (and football) to fellow followers of the game. He had no pretensions regarding literary merit; indeed, he never described himself as a poet, but signed his work 'A. C. Cricket Rhymester'. He was most associated with the Oval, hence his nickname, and sold thousands of copies of his swiftly executed rhymes and player profiles. Typical of his output is an 18-line tribute to a young Jack Hobbs, who had just scored 162 not out against Worcestershire at Surrey's home ground, which begins:

> Joy reigns supreme amongst the Surrey throng,
> Patrons break out in one triumphant song;
> Young Hobbs we loved as hero of today,
> Gaily he steers along his conquering way.

Such was Albert Craig's fame that shortly before his death in 1909 he received a message of goodwill from the Prince of Wales, later King George V.

STRIKING THE RIGHT NOTE

Many cricketers have had a musical bent. The Leicestershire all-rounder Ewart Astill, who played for England in the 1920s, would entertain teammates on the ukulele. Former New Zealand captain Jeremy Coney started out as a music teacher and can play several instruments. Alastair Cook was a child chorister who played the clarinet on the side. Ex-Indian opener Sanjay Manjrekar has sung professionally, releasing an album called *Rest Day* when his playing days were over. South African cricket virtuoso AB de Villiers also has an album to his name.

On the Caribbean beat, both Dwayne Bravo and Andre Russell have recorded singles. Since retiring from the first-class game in 2012, all-rounder Omari Banks has become a reggae star. Two West Indies top-liners, Curtly Ambrose and Richie Richardson, came together in retirement to form a band called the Big Bad Dread and the Bald Head, with Ambrose on bass, his one-time batting colleague on rhythm guitar.

The multi-faceted Brett Lee can add singing and guitar to his list of talents. Together with brother Shane (45 ODIs for Australia) and three other ex-cricketers, Lee formed a band called Six and Out. England batsman turned TV pundit Mark Butcher, who faced Brett Lee on numerous occasions, is a singer-songwriter with his own band. When his Surrey teammate Ben

Hollioake was killed in a car crash in 2002, Butcher movingly sang his own composition 'You're Never Gone' at the funeral.

TEN CRICKETING AUTOBIOGRAPHIES WITH EYE-CATCHING TITLES

You Guys Are History Devon Malcolm (England)

*Hands and Heals*Ian Healy (Australia)

Last in the Tin Bath David Lloyd (England)

Third Man to Fatty's Leg Steve James (England)

10 for 66 and All That Arthur Mailey (Australia)

Behind the Shades Duncan Fletcher (Zimbabwe)

Bootboy to President Brian Luckhurst (England)

I Don't Bruise Easily Brian Close (England)

Christmas in Raratonga John Wright (New Zealand)

Blood, Sweat and Treason Henry Olonga (Zimbabwe)

IT'S A FACT!

President George W. Bush was given a brief demonstration of cricket on the lawn of the US embassy in Islamabad during an official visit. He faced three deliveries from Inzamam-ul-Haq and managed not to be dismissed 'LBdubya'.

FEMALES OF THE SPECIES

> **❝** *I always thought I'd play cricket for Australia, I just never thought it would be in the women's team.* **❞**
>
> **CATHRYN FITZPATRICK, FAST BOWLER**

On 26 July 1745, a year before the Battle of Culloden, the *Reading Mercury* reported on a cricket match between 'eleven maids of Bramley and eleven maids of Hambleton'. The Hambleton maids came out on top by eight 'notches'. It is the first known account of the female side of the game.

The first women's 'county' match took place in 1811 between Surrey and Hampshire, though the event was staged in Middlesex. Two sporting noblemen underwrote the game to the tune of 1,000 guineas. It was not until 1887, however, that the first women's cricket club was founded, at Nun Appleton in Yorkshire. Three years later, 'The Original English Lady Cricketers' were divided into a Red XI and a Blue XI and played a number of exhibition games around the country. Their on-field strip was a white flannel blouse and long skirt, colour coded around the collar and hem and by a sash around the waist. In 1926, the Women's Cricket Association (WCA) was formed in England, and official organisations were established in Australia (1931) and New Zealand (1933). Other cricket-playing nations gradually followed suit after the war.

The first women's Test match took place between Australia and England at Brisbane in December 1934. It was first blood to England, who also won the second Test at Sydney and the three-match series 2–0, the final game ending in a draw. England's player of the series was Myrtle Maclagan, who took 7 for 10 with her off-breaks in Australia's inaugural innings (a record which stood until 1958). In the second match she became the first female Test centurion. The success of the women's team was in marked contrast to the fortunes of the men's side, which in England a few months before had surrendered the Ashes, prompting the *Morning Post* to publish the following quatrain:

> *What matter that we lost, mere nervy men*
> *Since England's women now play England's game,*
> *Wherefore Immortal* Wisden, *take your pen*
> *And write MACLAGAN on the scroll of fame.*

Australia toured England for the first time in 1937. It was a tight series, with one match apiece and the final Test drawn. England's Betty Snowball became the first woman to be run out for 99 in a Test match. Until 1960, these two countries, along with New Zealand, were the only Test-playing nations.

Inevitably, the ongoing tussle between England and Australia has been the principal focus, with the initiative swinging from one hemisphere to the other. Of the 21 series played between the two countries to date, Australia has won eight, England six and seven have been drawn. When England came out on top in 2005, it was their first series victory over the old enemy for 42 years.

THE ASHES

In 1998, what had always been unofficially understood became official: the two countries would now compete for the Ashes trophy, and unlike the men's version there was to be no doubt as to the provenance of the incinerated remains. At a formal ceremony at Lord's a miniature bat, signed by the England and Australian teams, and a copy of the WCA constitution and rules book were consigned to the flames. A trophy made of wood from an ancient yew tree is the Ashes' sealed resting place.

In 2013, for the first time, the Ashes series was contested across all three formats of the game on the basis of a points system: the single Test counting for six points, the three ODIs two points each, and the three Twenty20 games a further two points apiece. The Test match was drawn, but England regained the Ashes, lost two years earlier, on the strength of a convincing 5–1 victory in the shorter formats.

England retained the Ashes the following winter, but in 2015 fortunes were once again reversed. Australia won the only Test (with the points now reduced from six to four) and two of the three ODIs, England taking the Twenty20 series by the same margin. It was 10–6 to Australia, and the Ashes headed back Down Under.

WORLD CUPS

The first Women's ODI World Cup was staged in England in 1973, beating the men to a tournament by two years. With not enough countries to go round, an International XI competed to make up the numbers. It was a round-robin format with England and Australia playing the last scheduled match, which in effect became the final. The home side won. In the nine World Cup tournaments since then, Australia has lifted the trophy six times, England twice. New Zealand, on home ground in 2000, has been the only exception to the rule.

England were champions in the first ICC Women's Twenty20 World Cup, defeating New Zealand in the final at Lord's in 2009, pace bowler Katherine Brunt taking a match-winning 3 for 6. The 2010, 2012 and 2014 tournaments were won by Australia, but they failed to make it four in a row when they lost to the West Indies in the 2016 final at Kolkata.

> ## IT'S A FACT!
>
> An international at cricket and football, Ellyse Perry is the first woman to represent Australia in World Cups in two sports. An outstanding all-rounder in all three cricketing formats, she is also a key defender for the Australian national soccer team and for Sydney FC.

TURNING PRO

England's women cricketers moved closer to their male counterparts in 2014 when the ECB awarded central contracts to 18 players. A year later the Middlesex batsman Fran Wilson was added to the list of contracted professionals.

Another major development followed in 2016 with the launch of the first Women's Cricket Super League, initially comprising six teams in a Twenty20 competition (the serpentine Southern Vipers were the inaugural winners). A 50-overs version is in the pipeline. It's all a far cry from the voluminous skirts and gentle deliveries of 200 years ago.

TWELVE OF THE BEST

🏏 MYRTLE MACLAGAN (ENGLAND)

In her 14-Test career (1934–51) Myrtle Maclagan scored just over 1,000 runs and took 60 wickets. She regularly opened the batting with Betty Snowball, the media dubbing them the Hobbs and Sutcliffe of women's cricket. Her bowling was a versatile mix of seam and off-spin.

BETTY WILSON (AUSTRALIA)

The first cricketer of either sex to make a century and take ten wickets in the same Test. It happened at Melbourne against England in 1958. Wilson scored exactly 100 in Australia's second innings and with the ball took 7 for 7 and 4 for 9. Her match figures of 11 for 16 included the first women's Test hat-trick.

ENID BAKEWELL (ENGLAND)

Bakewell scored a century on her debut in 1968 against Australia – the first of four she made in 12 Tests. She scored a half-century in each innings of a Test on four occasions and was the first to register back-to-back hundreds. No less effective with the ball, her left-arm spin harvested 50 Test wickets at an economical 16 runs apiece.

RACHAEL HEYHOE-FLINT (ENGLAND)

In an international career spanning two decades, Rachael Heyhoe-Flint won 22 Test caps and played in 23 ODIs. During the 11 years in which she captained England in Tests (1966–77), the side remained undefeated. She was the first woman to hit a six in a Test match and led her country to victory in the inaugural World Cup in 1973.

DIANA EDULJI (INDIA)

The Mumbai-born Diana Edulji played in India's first Test match, against the West Indies at Bangalore in 1976. A very effective left-arm orthodox spinner, she took 63 Test wickets and a further 46 in ODIs. She captained her country in both formats of the game and for the best part of 17 years was India's most outstanding woman cricketer.

BELINDA CLARK (AUSTRALIA)

Clark held the Australian record for the most runs both in Test matches (919) and ODIs (4,844), averaging over 45 in each format. Her 118 ODI appearances was another record. Thirteen years before Sachin Tendulkar emulated the feat, she scored a double century in an ODI (229 not out against Denmark in 1997). She captained Australia to victory in the 1997 and 2005 World Cups.

JAN BRITTIN (ENGLAND)

The Surrey right-hander set new records in both the long and short forms of the game. She scored ten centuries in her 27 Tests and 63 ODIs (five in each format). In 1984, she became the first woman cricketer to score over 500 runs in a calendar year, and in 1998 made back-to-back Test hundreds against Australia, including a career-best 167.

EMILY DRUMM (NEW ZEALAND)

Emily Drumm made her Test debut at the age of 17. She played five Tests in all, scoring two centuries and two fifties in six innings and finishing with an average of 144.33. She appeared in 101 ODIs, captaining her country in 41 of them. Her greatest triumph was leading New Zealand to victory in the 2000 World Cup.

CLAIRE TAYLOR (ENGLAND)

An outstanding performer with the bat, Taylor scored centuries in consecutive Tests against South Africa in 2003 (177 and 131). Three years later in an ODI against India at Lord's she made 156, one of a record eight hundreds in ODIs. In 2009, she became the first woman to be selected as one of *Wisden*'s Five Cricketers of the Year.

MITHALI RAJ (INDIA)

In only her third Test, against England at Taunton in 2002, the 19-year-old Mithali Raj scored a record 214. She is by far her country's most prolific run-scorer in ODIs and one of the highest-ranked internationals. In 2005 she led India to their first World Cup final and a year later to their first ever Test series win in England.

CATHRYN FITZPATRICK (AUSTRALIA)

At around 120 kph (75 mph), Cathryn Fitzpatrick was cricket's fastest female bowler. Her disconcerting pace helped Australia to victory in the 1997 and 2005 World Cups, and her career haul of 180 wickets in ODIs (average 16.79) set a world record. She took a further 60 wickets in her 13 Test appearances, the last of them against India in 2006.

CHARLOTTE EDWARDS (ENGLAND)

England's charismatic captain led from the front, scoring four centuries in Test matches and more than twice that number in ODIs. To add to that are the 66 wickets she captured with her leg-breaks. In 2009, she led England to victory in both the ODI

World Cup and ICC Twenty20, and captained the side that triumphantly regained the Ashes in 2013.

PLAYING THE MEN'S GAME

- England wicketkeeper-batsman Sarah Taylor became the first woman to play in an A-grade match in Australia, when she turned out for Northern Districts against Port Adelaide in 2015. Taylor didn't bat in the game but took two alert catches behind the stumps.

- Australian pace bowler Zoe Goss, playing for the Bradman XI against a World XI at the Sydney Cricket Ground in 1994, dismissed West Indian stars Brian Lara and Jeffrey Dujon.

- In 2015, England quickie Kate Cross became the first woman to play in the Central Lancashire League in its 123-year history. She made her presence felt by taking 8 for 47 for Heywood against Unsworth.

- England batsman Arran Brindle registered the first female century in men's Premier League cricket, scoring 128 for Louth v Market Deeping in 2011.

DOWN TO THE WIRE

··

> *The key to handling pressure is to enjoy it.*
> **STEVE WAUGH, FORMER AUSTRALIAN CAPTAIN**

No one who saw the final dramatic stages of the Edgbaston Test against Australia in 2005, when England scraped home by two runs, is likely to forget it in a hurry. Or the match at Cardiff four years later, when Monty Panesar and James Anderson defied the Australian attack for 50 interminable minutes to gain an honourable draw for the home side. Or the stunning climax to the Twenty20 World Cup final at Kolkata in 2016, when Carlos Brathwaite powered the West Indies to the trophy.

It was cricket at its gripping best and had spectators perched on the edge of their seats – as did these other games that went down to the wire.

VITAL RUN

The first Test between South Africa and England at Durban in 1948. South Africa, batting first, totalled a modest 161.

England's two opening bowlers, Alec Bedser of Surrey and Cliff Gladwin of Derbyshire, shared seven wickets between them. Len Hutton (83) and Denis Compton (72) were the top scorers in England's reply of 253 – a useful first-innings lead of 92.

When the home side was dismissed for just 219 in their second innings, the match seemed to be in the bag: only 128 required for victory. But England lost wickets steadily. They were 52 for 3, then 70 for 6, with only the tail left. The man who had done the damage was South Africa's debutant fast bowler Cuan McCarthy. The 19-year-old from Natal finished with figures of 6 for 43, which would prove to be his best Test return.

When Gladwin joined Bedser at the wicket the score was 116 for 8. Twelve more runs were needed to win. By the start of the final (eight-ball) over, to be bowled by Lindsay Tuckett, the target had been whittled down to eight runs. Bedser brought the scores level off the sixth ball, with any one of four results still possible. Gladwin had a heave at the seventh ball but missed it entirely.

The two batsmen conferred mid-pitch and decided to run on the next ball, come what may. As Tuckett ran in to bowl the fielders closed in ready to prevent a single. Gladwin had another fruitless swipe at the ball, which rapped him on the pad and bounced a yard or two in front of him. The bespectacled South African spinner 'Tufty' Mann lunged at it from short leg, but not quickly enough. Bedser and Gladwin, neither of whom was known for his agility, scampered through for the vital run. England were the victors by two wickets.

IT'S A FACT!

England's opening pair against New Zealand at Headingley in 1958, Arthur Milton and M. J. K. Smith, were both double internationals – Milton at football, Smith at rugby union. There have been none since.

MAKING HISTORY

The first match in the 1960–61 Test series between Australia and the West Indies took place at the Gabba in Brisbane. The visitors posted 453 in their first innings, Garry Sobers contributing 132. Australia's reply of 505 included an innings of 181 from Norman O'Neill. The West Indies scored 284 second time around, leaving Australia a target of 233 in 310 minutes. When Alan Davidson was run out for 80 (having become the first player to complete a match double of ten wickets and 100 runs in a Test) with the score at 226 for 7, Australia seem poised for victory.

When the last (eight-ball) over began they needed six runs to win. The ferocious Wes Hall stood ready at the end of his long run-up. A sharp single was taken off the first ball, then Australian captain Richie Benaud mistimed a hook and was caught by wicketkeeper Alexander for 52. New batsman Ian Meckiff defended the third ball and scampered through for a bye off the fourth. His partner Wally Grout ballooned the next delivery towards backward square leg, where Rohan Kanhai shaped to take the catch, only to find himself competing with the excitable bowler; the ball fell to the ground between them. Meanwhile, the batsmen crossed: three runs needed.

A perfect 80-yard (73-m) throw from Conrad Hunte on the mid-wicket boundary ran out Grout off the sixth ball, but not before the batsmen had run two. The scores were level with two balls to go. Lindsey Kline clipped his first ball to square leg and ran. Joe Solomon calmly gathered the ball and with one stump to aim at broke the wicket. After 502 matches Test cricket had its first tie.

MOPPING UP

Spectators had the English weather to thank for injecting drama into the last Test between England and Australia at the Oval in 1968. The match situation at lunch on the final day was England 494 (John Edrich 164, Basil D'Oliveira 158) and 181, Australia 324 (Bill Lawry 135) and 86 for 5. Australia required a further 266 to win, an unlikely prospect with only two sessions and five wickets remaining. However, having won the first Test and with the next three drawn, Australia would take the series if their batsmen could hold out for the rest of the day.

Rain drove the players off the field one minute before lunch, and during the interval a freak storm completely flooded the playing area. As the sun broke through, the ground staff began mopping-up operations, joined by volunteers from the crowd, who helped to lay scores of absorbent sacks and then squeezed them dry beyond the boundary rope. Play finally resumed at 4.45 p.m., and until D'Oliveira bowled wicketkeeper Barry Jarman 39 minutes later, it seemed that Australia would succeed in saving the match. England captain Colin Cowdrey brought back his Kent colleague Derek Underwood to bowl from the pavilion end. With his first and sixth balls he dismissed Ashley Mallett and Graham McKenzie, respectively. Twenty minutes later, with the fielders closing in, John Gleeson became the next victim. Then, with a few minutes to go, opener John Inverarity padded up to Underwood's 'arm ball', having batted through the innings, and was given out LBW. England had won by 226 runs, Underwood 7 for 50.

IT'S A FACT!

In 1981, the Middlesex batsman Roland Butcher became the first black cricketer to win an England cap. He made his debut in the third Test against the West Indies at Barbados, where he was born.

GLOOMY ENDING

In July 1971, Lancashire met Gloucestershire in the semi-final of the Gillette Cup at Old Trafford in front of a crowd of 24,000, with millions more watching on television. The visitors batted first and made 229 for 6 in their 60 overs, the South African all-rounder Mike Procter top scorer with 65.

Set to make just under four runs an over to win, Lancashire began steadily, their England opening pair of David Lloyd and Barry Wood putting on 61 for the first wicket. West Indies captain

Clive Lloyd contributed a useful 34, but wickets continued to fall, and with five overs in the match remaining, the home side, with just three wickets left, needed 25 runs for victory.

It was nearly 9.00 p.m. (an hour after lunch was lost through rain) and there were no floodlights, though the lights were on in the pavilion and in the surrounding streets. In the advancing gloom, Gloucestershire captain Tony Brown threw the ball to former England off-spinner John Mortimore, who already had three wickets to his name.

Batsman David Hughes briefly conferred with his own skipper Jack Bond, the non-striker, before shaping to face the first ball of the 56th over. He hit it for six and then followed with four, two, two, four and six – twenty-four runs off the over. By now it was so dark that many in the crowd (and on the field) were unable to see where the ball was hit but were guided by the cheers of those who could. The winning run, struck by Bond, came off the fifth ball of the next over and Lancashire were home by three wickets. Six weeks later they lifted the Gillette Cup at Lord's.

DRESSING DOWN

At close of play on the second day of the county match between Hampshire and Nottinghamshire at Southampton in May 1930, the home side required just one run to win. The extra half hour had been taken, but the Nottinghamshire captain A. W. Carr refused to continue beyond that, even though victory for his opponents was a formality. The next morning the Nottinghamshire side took to the field in their travelling clothes, a couple of the players wearing overcoats to ward off the chill. The winning run was mercifully struck off the second ball of the day.

IN A SPIN

Rain had reduced the County Championship match between Sussex and Surrey at Eastbourne in August 1972 to little more than two days. But in front of a holiday crowd both teams did their best to keep the game alive. Surrey, batting first, scored 300 for 4 before declaring. Then sporting declarations by both captains set up a run chase for the home side of 205 in 135 minutes to win. A big second-wicket partnership between Geoffrey Greenidge and Roger Prideaux (who had made a century in the first innings) took Sussex to 187 for 1, with three overs remaining. Eighteen to get, at a run a ball, seemed a formality.

With the first ball of the next over, the Surrey and England off-spinner Pat Pocock bowled Greenidge: 187 for 2. His third ball bowled Mike Buss and, after conceding two runs from the fourth, he caught and bowled Jim Parks off the last. It was 189 for 4. Eleven runs came off the following over bowled by Robin Jackman. Sussex needed five runs from the final over with Prideaux (97 not out) on strike.

Pocock dismissed Prideaux with the first ball and Griffith with the second, completing a hat-trick. Five runs were required from four balls with four wickets standing. The new batsman Jeremy Morley was stumped off the next ball and Pocock had taken four in four and six in nine (a world record). A run came from the fourth ball, then Tony Buss was bowled by the fifth. Off the last ball of the game Uday Joshi was run out going for a second run – match drawn, with Sussex 202 for 9 at the close. It was the first time that five wickets had fallen in a final over, with Pocock's seven wickets (for four runs) in 11 balls yet another world record.

HONOURS EVEN

The inaugural Test between Zimbabwe and England was staged at the Queen's Sports Club, Bulawayo, in December 1996. The home side, batting first and keen to make their mark against an experienced England side, scored 376. Wicketkeeper Andy Flower top scored with 112, brother Grant chipping in with 43. England made a solid response with centuries from Nasser Hussain (113) and John Crawley (112), but lost their last six wickets for 78, finishing on 406.

Four wickets from spinner Phil Tufnell restricted Zimbabwe to 234 in their second innings, leaving England to chase down 205 in 37 overs. Mike Atherton, England's captain, went cheaply. But a second-wicket stand between Nick Knight and Alec Stewart put on 137 before the latter departed the scene. Hussain didn't trouble the scorers; Crawley was dismissed for seven and Graham Thorpe for two. At the other end Knight continued to flourish, despite Zimbabwe's negative tactic of bowling wide of the stumps, a manoeuvre that went unchecked by the umpires.

Thirteen were needed from Heath Streak's final over. The first two balls yielded two runs. Knight swung the third delivery for six over deep square leg. The next ball was so far outside the off stump that the batsman had no chance of reaching it, but it was not given as a wide. The fifth, driven to long-off, brought two more runs. One ball to go, three runs needed. Knight clubbed it into the covers; the batsmen ran two but failed to complete a third run, Stuart Carlisle's throw beating the England opener to the line. He had made 96, and for the first time in Test history a match was drawn with the scores level.

CUP NERVES

Edgbaston was the venue for the second semi-final of the 1999 World Cup: Australia v South Africa. Australia lost the toss and were put in to bat. At 68 for 4 South Africa were decidedly on top, but a partnership of 90 between captain Steve Waugh (56) and Michael Bevan (65) helped the Aussies to a respectable 213 from their 50 overs. South Africa's pace bowlers did most of the damage, Shaun Pollock taking 5 for 36, Allan Donald 4 for 32.

The South African innings followed a remarkably similar pattern to that of their opponents. The Proteas were 61 for 4 (3 of them to Shane Warne) before Jacques Kallis (53) and Jonty Rhodes (43) put on 84 together. Pollock added a further valuable 20 runs, and when he was the seventh batsman out the score stood at 183. Thirty-one required to win (a tie would see Australia through to the final as they had the better record in the Super Sixes). Importantly for South Africa, the destructive Lance Klusener was still there.

Two more wickets fell: Mark Boucher bowled by Glenn McGrath and Steve Elworthy run out. Allan Donald was last man in. Nine runs were required as Damien Fleming began the final over. Klusener smashed the first two balls to the boundary, levelling the scores with still four deliveries to go. He mishit the fourth ball to Mark Waugh at mid-off and galloped down the pitch for what would be the winning run. Donald, who had narrowly missed being run out the ball before, was slow to move. Waugh threw the ball to Fleming, who rolled it to wicketkeeper Adam Gilchrist at the other end. The tardy Donald, dropping his bat in the excitement, was stranded midway. Australia were through to the final.

MYSTERY AND MENACE

> *Stuff that stiff upper lip crap.*
> *Let's see how stiff it is when it's split.*
>
> **JEFF THOMSON, AUSTRALIAN FAST BOWLER**

Down the years the game has produced some mesmerising spin bowlers and some speedsters of alarming pace and venom. Here are a few of each.

ALBERT MOLD

Lancashire's Albert Mold (he was actually born in Northamptonshire) was one of the deadliest fast bowlers of his day. On 18 occasions he took eight wickets or more in an innings; 14 times he took thirteen or more in a match. He achieved a hat-trick twice in his first-class career and once took four wickets in four balls. Playing against Surrey in 1896, he clean bowled England's George Lohmann, despatching the bail nearly 58 m (63 yd 6 in). Throughout his career, however, batsmen questioned the legality of his delivery, claiming that Mold threw the ball. Matters came to a head in a county match against Somerset at Old Trafford in 1901, when umpire James Phillips no-balled Mold 16 times in ten overs. A meeting of county captains shortly afterwards confirmed this judgement by a vote of 11 to 1. Albert Mold's first-class career was over, and many batsmen quietly breathed a sigh of relief.

B. J. T. BOSANQUET

The Middlesex all-rounder invented the googly (an off-break bowled with a leg-break action) while playing a table game called Twisti-Twosti, the object of which was to bounce a tennis ball out of reach of the opponent seated opposite. He unleashed his mystery ball in a county match against Leicestershire in 1900. The ball bounced four times before reaching the batsman Sammy Coe, who was stumped, in more ways than one, for 98. Two years later Bosanquet was a member of the first MCC side to tour Australia. In the match against New South Wales he clean bowled the great Victor Trumper with the first ever googly seen in Australia. Thereafter, the googly was known Down Under as a 'Bosie'. Bosanquet played in just seven Test matches, taking 25 wickets in all, but his legacy to the game is immeasurable. He later said of his devious delivery, 'It was not unfair; only immoral.'

IT'S A FACT!

In 2013, South Africa's Graeme Smith became the first cricketer from any country to captain his side in 100 Tests.

HAROLD LARWOOD

Larwood will always be remembered as the main man in England's 'bodyline' attack of 1932–33. In that series against Australia, Larwood's 33 wickets came at under 20 runs apiece. His battered opponents were more inclined to count the bruises. A former pit boy in the Nottinghamshire coalfields, Larwood was no more than medium height but had wide shoulders and long arms. A perfectly balanced sideways action enabled him to generate extreme pace and accuracy. He returned from Australia a popular hero, but moves were already afoot to ban leg-theory bowling and Larwood was made the scapegoat. He was asked to sign a letter apologising for his role on the tour but refused and never played for England again. For a few more years he continued to wreak havoc on the county circuit. Then, in 1950, Larwood left the country that had dishonoured him and with his family moved to Australia, where, ironically, he was warmly welcomed.

YANKEE MASTER

John Barton King, one of the finest bowlers of his time and by some distance America's greatest cricketer, was born in Philadelphia. His extremely effective bowling action, developed from playing baseball as a child, enabled him to swing the ball both ways at considerable pace. In the final strides of his run-up he held the ball above his head with both hands in the manner of a baseball pitcher. He successfully toured England three times with the Gentlemen of Philadelphia, once bowling the great Ranjitsinhji first ball. On his final tour in 1908, he topped the English bowling averages with 87 wickets (in just ten matches) at 11 runs apiece.

JACK IVERSON

Iverson made a sensational impact in his brief career in Australian cricket. He was 34 before he made his first-class debut for Victoria and was picked for Australia a year later. He made five Test appearances, all in the 1950–51 series against England, taking 21 wickets at an average of 15.23. It was while serving with the army in New Guinea during the Second World War that Iverson, who started out as a pace bowler, developed a new method of spinning the ball. Gripping it between his thumb and bent middle finger, he was able to bowl off-breaks, leg-breaks and googlies without any discernible change of action. It was enough to fool most of the England batsmen much of the time. In the third Test at Sydney his 6 for 27 saw the opposition reduced to 123 in their second innings. An ankle injury later in the series ended a remarkable career that was over almost before it began.

FRANK TYSON

'Typhoon' Tyson burst onto the English cricket scene in the early 1950s. The Lancashire-born fast bowler signed up for

Northamptonshire and made an immediate impact, not least with the slip cordon which promptly repositioned itself several yards further back. It was jokingly said that Tyson at the start of his excessively long run-up could barely see the wicketkeeper in the distance. What was certainly true was that batsmen often barely sighted the ball. He was chosen ahead of Fred Trueman to tour Australia in 1954–55 and in the first Test at Brisbane, which the visitors lost by an innings, his figures were 1 for 160. After that it was all England – and Tyson! In the next Test at Sydney his 10 wickets in the match paved the way for an England victory. He followed this with another match-winning performance of 7 for 27 in Australia's second innings at Melbourne. Plagued by injuries, Frank Tyson made only 17 Test appearances, but he made sure they counted.

ABDUL QADIR

It helped that with his thick black locks and short pointed beard (grown at the suggestion of Pakistan captain Imran Khan to enhance the mystique), Abdul Qadir at times resembled a stage magician. For a decade starting in the late 1970s he was the world's foremost 'leggie'. His spinner's guile was combined with a fast bowler's aggression, reflected in his extravagant follow-through. Bowling a mixture of leg-spin and googlies (of which he had two versions) and the occasional flipper (a ball which gains pace off the pitch and stays low), the magical Qadir was more than a handful for most batsmen. At the Oval in 1987 he took ten wickets in the match. A few months later at Lahore, in the next Test between the two countries, he bamboozled

England's batsmen to the tune of 9 for 56 in the first innings, adding four more wickets in the second. His haul for the three-match series was a bewildering 30.

CHARLIE GRIFFITH

The West Indies have produced few pace bowlers as frighteningly fast as 'The Bajun Express'. His new-ball partnership with Wes Hall was the most feared in world cricket. Griffith, a little under 2 metres tall and powerfully built, stormed up to the wicket and delivered the ball with a chest-on action that led to accusations of throwing. His most deadly delivery was a blisteringly fast yorker – aside, that is, from his head-high bouncer, one of which nearly killed the Indian captain Nari Contractor during a match against Griffith's native Barbados. In England in 1963, and despite one or two heroic innings from the home batsmen, he blew away the opposition, taking 32 wickets in the series and 119 on the tour as a whole (at an average of under 13). Unlike his partner Hall, an amiable man without ball in hand, Griffith came across as a threateningly surly character. It didn't hurt the image.

IT'S A FACT!

Pakistani fast bowler Wasim Akram achieved a hat-trick in successive Test matches against Sri Lanka in 1998–99.

PAUL ADAMS

South Africa's Paul Adams had one of the most contorted bowling actions ever seen in the first-class game. At the moment of delivery, the back of his head faced the batsman and his eyes appeared to be looking skyward. His distorted, whirring action was memorably described as resembling a 'frog in a blender'. Nevertheless, for a while, it proved successful enough. Adams made his Test debut at Port Elizabeth on Boxing Day 1995, after only five first-class matches for Western Province. A couple of weeks short of his 19th birthday, he was the youngest cricketer to represent South Africa. Bowling 'chinamen' (the left-armer's off-break to a right-hander), he took 35 wickets in his first three Test series. But as his bowling action became less of a distraction and the lack of variety in his repertoire left him exposed, his fortunes faded. In 2004 he took the last of his 134 Test wickets. No South African left-arm spinner has taken more.

JEFF THOMSON

'Thommo's' Test debut – against Pakistan at Melbourne in 1972–73 – went largely unnoticed. Playing with a broken bone in his foot (a fact he kept from the selectors) may have had something to do with it. Recalled to the side to play England two years later, he made an altogether different impression. In the first Test at Brisbane, bowling on a pitch that was underprepared because of bad weather, he reached speeds of close to 160 kph (100 mph) and made the ball lift alarmingly. His slingy action was like that of a javelin thrower, with the ball whipped out from behind his back as he reached the stumps. He and Dennis Lillee formed one of the greatest ever pace partnerships, destroying and demoralising opposition batsmen the world over: 'Ashes to ashes, dust to dust, if Thommo don't get ya, then Lillee must.' In 51 Tests spanning 12 years, Thomson took exactly 200 wickets. With fewer injuries he could have had many more.

AJANTHA MENDIS

Mendis added his own brand of mystery to that of the Sri Lankan maestro Muttiah Muralitharan. Bowling in tandem against India at Colombo in 2008, the pair took 19 wickets between them (Mendis taking 8 on his Test debut), spinning Sri Lanka to a crushing victory by an innings and 239 runs. The young spinner went on to take 26 wickets in the three-match series, collecting the scalps of India's great quartet – Dravid, Tendulkar, Laxman and Ganguly – in the process. His mixture of off-breaks, googlies, top-spinners and 'carrom balls' (a finger-flicked leg-break which derives its name from a popular board game in the subcontinent) frequently wrong-footed the batsmen. And, of course, it helped to have Murali bowling at the other end. As batsmen have learned to 'read' Mendis his effectiveness at Test level has diminished, though he continues to have success in the shorter formats. He'll just have to come up with another mystery ball.

IT'S A FACT!

The poet Laurie Lee (author of *Cider with Rosie*) was hit on the head by an airborne beer bottle while watching Australia v New Zealand at the Sydney Cricket Ground in 1974. Lee, who was knocked unconscious and required several stitches, had been sitting among the raucous crowd on the ground's notorious 'Hill'.

MEN IN WHITE COATS

" Doubt? When I'm umpiring there's never any doubt. "
FRANK CHESTER, ENGLISH UMPIRE

For most cricket matches outside the professional game the tradition is to have two umpires, one supplied by each side. Partisan feelings should be suppressed in the interests of impartiality, though human nature being what it is umpires will occasionally let their preferences and prejudices get the better of them.

In 1992, to eliminate accusations of bias at Test level (and particularly in Pakistan, where umpiring controversies had become endemic), the ICC appointed one neutral umpire to stand in each match. Ten years later neutrality was extended to both umpires, to be drawn from an elite panel that would serve Test cricket around the world. The number of umpires on duty in modern Test matches has swelled to four: two on the field, a third to adjudicate with the help of video replays, and a fourth who takes care of the match balls and the welfare of his three colleagues.

UMPIRES GO HIGH-TECH

A number of technological devices have been devised to help umpires make the right decision.

LIGHT METER:

A digital instrument designed to give accurate readings of light levels on the field. The umpire stands at one end of the pitch and points the meter towards the sightscreen to take the reading.

HAWK-EYE:

A computerised system that tracks the trajectory of the ball via several strategically placed cameras, used by the third umpire to rule on LBW decisions.

SNICKOMETER:

Visual sound waves emanating from a stump microphone help determine whether the ball has touched the bat on the way through to the wicketkeeper or close fielders.

HOT SPOT:

An infra-red imaging system that shows, by means of a bright white spot, the extent of any contact between bat and ball.

TV REPLAYS:

Slow-motion replays from a variety of angles that can assist the umpire in adjudicating on stumpings, run-outs, catches and boundaries.

ONE-ARMED UMPIRE

Frank Chester raised umpiring standards to a new level. His promising career as an all-rounder with Worcestershire (at 17 he became the youngest player to score a century in a county match) was cruelly terminated by the First World War: severely wounded while serving in Salonika, his right arm was amputated just below the elbow. Undeterred, he became a first-class umpire and stood in 48 Tests (at a time when there were far fewer matches than today), winning the respect of players around the world. He was the first umpire to bend low over the stumps to obtain a better view as the bowler delivered the ball. Throughout his career he counted the balls per over with the same six pebbles he had gathered from his mother's garden prior to standing in his first match.

IT'S A FACT!

The former West Indian umpire Steve Bucknor stood in a record 128 Test matches, 20 more than his nearest rival, South Africa's Rudi Koertzen.

UMPIRE IN DISTRESS

The English umpire Arthur Fagg refused to take to the field on the third morning of the second Test against the West Indies at Edgbaston in 1973, and threatened to withdraw from the match altogether, because of dissent shown the previous day by some of the West Indian players, among them captain Rohan Kanhai. Fagg claimed he had been verbally abused after turning down an appeal for caught behind against Geoffrey Boycott in England's first innings. For one over his place was taken by ex-England all-rounder and former first-class umpire Alan Oakman, at the time the Warwickshire coach and conveniently on hand. An embarrassing escalation of the incident was avoided when apologies were made, allowing Fagg to resume his duties.

The ex-Kent and England opening batsman (the only player to have scored a double century in each innings of a first-class match, a feat he performed in 1938) was generally well regarded as an umpire, officiating in 18 Tests and 7 ODIs before retiring for health reasons. His stand at Edgbaston (or rather his refusal to do so) caused something of a sensation, but the media and cricketing public for the most part supported the beleaguered man in the white coat.

IT'S A FACT!

The first Test match to be televised was England v Australia at Lord's in 1938.

WATER SPORT

During the 1955–56 MCC tour of Pakistan, seven of the English team, including captain Donald Carr, kidnapped the Pakistani umpire Idris Baig at his hotel in Peshawar and carted him across town for a spot of 'water torture'. Placing him in a chair at their own residence, they offered their teetotal victim a glass of whisky before pouring two buckets of cold water over his head. The reason for these unruly hijinks was, as the players saw it, Baig's pompous manner and his bias in favour of the home side when officiating out in the middle. Unsurprisingly, the incident caused outrage in the Pakistani camp and media. A. H. Kardar, their captain and a former teammate of Carr at Oxford University, was particularly incensed. Only the intervention of the MCC president, Field Marshal Alexander of Tunis, prevented the cancellation of the tour. Despite the apparent black mark, Donald Carr went on to manage several England tours overseas and became a senior administrator in the sport.

FINGERING THE UMPIRE

A heated exchange between England captain Mike Gatting and Pakistani umpire Shakoor Rana on the second day of the Faisalabad Test in 1987 nearly brought the tour to an end. The umpire accused Gatting of cheating, saying he had adjusted the field placings while off-spinner Eddie Hemmings was running into bowl. Earlier Gatting had implied that Rana, who provocatively sported a Pakistan sweater under his white coat (though unlike his brothers Shafqat and Azmat he never played at Test level), was biased in his rulings. Both men angrily waved a finger in each other's face, following which the umpire refused to take any further part in the game unless he received a fulsome apology. For the sake of the tour and cricket itself, Gatting complied. He was not the first Test captain to have had a run-in with Rana. Four years earlier at Karachi, New Zealand skipper Jeremy Coney threatened to lead his players off the field after a controversial decision by the umpire. Despite all this, Shakoor Rana continued as a Test umpire until 1996.

IT'S A FACT!

Umpire Syd Buller collapsed and died in the pavilion at Edgbaston during the county match between Warwickshire and Nottinghamshire in 1970, having just brought the players off the field because of rain.

UMPIRE'S SIGNALS

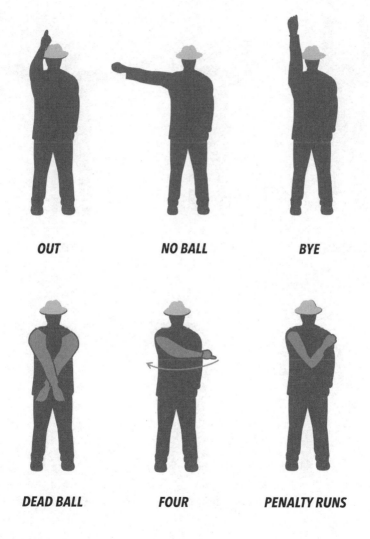

OUT NO BALL BYE

DEAD BALL FOUR PENALTY RUNS

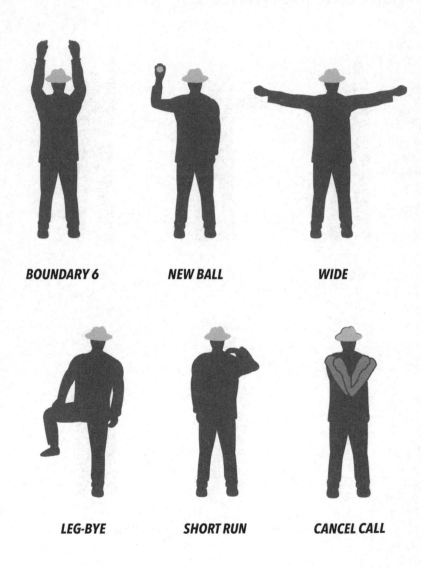

BOUNDARY 6   **NEW BALL**   **WIDE**

LEG-BYE   **SHORT RUN**   **CANCEL CALL**

NOT PLAYING THE GAME

. . . .

The psychology of the game is accurately condensed in these few words: 'It's not cricket'.
LORD HARRIS, KENT AND ENGLAND CAPTAIN

'Play up! play up! and play the game!' is a much-quoted line from Sir Henry Newbolt's patriotic poem 'Vitai Lampada'. But it's a sentiment that has not always been followed in cricket. Gamesmanship, bad behaviour on the field and political manoeuvrings off it have sometimes sabotaged the spirit of the summer game and, on occasions, stopped it being played at all.

TACTICAL ERROR

Worcestershire and Somerset met in a Group A fixture during the 1979 Benson & Hedges 55-overs competition. The match had been scheduled for the day before, but rain at New Road had delayed the start. Somerset, as leaders of their group, were on course for a place in the quarter-final, but in the end it could all come down to which team had the best strike rate. In order to preserve Somerset's current standing in that regard, their captain and opening batsman Brian Rose declared his side's innings closed after one over, with the score at one (a no-ball). Worcestershire, in the form of their New Zealand player Glenn Turner, then scored the necessary two runs to win and the match was over in a matter of minutes.

Angry spectators, including many Somerset supporters who had made the long journey up the M5 in anticipation of a keenly fought contest, expressed their displeasure. Rose was widely condemned in the media, though he remained unrepentant, claiming that he had acted strictly within the rules. However, his success at manipulating the result was short-lived. At a specially convened meeting of the Test and County Cricket Board a few days later, Somerset was expelled from the competition for not conforming to the spirit of the game. Two years later they lifted the Benson & Hedges trophy at Lord's, unquestionable champions.

IT'S A FACT!

In the Test against Pakistan at Perth in 1979, Australian opener Alan Hilditch was controversially given out, having 'handled the ball'. As the non-striker, he had picked up a wayward return and helpfully handed the ball to the bowler Sarfraz Nawaz, who unsportingly appealed. The umpire had no choice but to give the batsman out.

LILLEE'S CLANGER

Australian pace man Dennis Lillee found himself the centre of attention on the fourth day of the first Test against England at Perth in 1979, only this time as a batsman not a bowler. Lillee arrived at the crease sporting an aluminium bat, a promotional stunt for a friend who manufactured them. There was nothing in the rules of the game prohibiting the use of aluminium bats, but that was because cricket's governing body had never anticipated such a thing. One man who didn't approve was the Australian captain Greg Chappell, watching from the dressing room and annoyed that the metallic bat slowed down potential boundary-scoring shots. Meanwhile, his opposite number on the field, Mike Brearley, complained to the umpires that the bat had damaged the ball.

Chappell dispatched 12th man Rodney Hogg to the middle with a conventional willow and instructions for Lillee to make a swap. But the fast bowler refused. Play was held up for almost 10 minutes while the batsman, umpires and the England captain remonstrated with one another, and the matter was only resolved when Chappell himself entered the fray and insisted that Lillee give up the aluminium bat, which he did with ill grace, hurling it metres away. The game recommenced, and Lillee, whose metallurgic escapade lasted just four balls, went on to make 19 before delivering commentators their dream dismissal: 'Lillee, caught Willey, bowled Dilley'.

SIX OF THE BEST

The man at the centre of the storm was match referee Mike Denness, a former England captain. He was officiating at the second Test between South Africa and India at Port Elizabeth in 2001, and during the course of the game cited six Indian players for misconduct. Three of them – spinner Harbhajan Singh, batsman Shiv Sunder Das and wicketkeeper Deep Dasgupta – received suspended one-match bans for excessive appealing. Virender Sehwag was banned for one Test for aggressively claiming a catch off Jacques Kallis when the ball had patently bounced in front of him, and the captain Sourav Ganguly received a similar penalty for not controlling his team.

But the most controversial citing was that of Sachin Tendulkar for ball tampering. The television cameras had captured Tendulkar picking at the seam of the ball when bowling, though he claimed to be merely cleaning it (an action to which he should have drawn the umpire's attention). Uproar broke out, with India's cricket board at loggerheads with the ICC, who backed their match referee. There were accusations of racism, and when the Indian and South African boards usurped the ICC's role and replaced Denness for the next Test, the ICC designated the match 'unofficial'. In India, effigies of Denness were burned in the streets and there were threats of cancelling the forthcoming tour of England. In the event, the bans issued to Tendulkar and Ganguly were lifted, with only Sehwag having to sit out the next Test.

10 OTHER THINGS THAT HAVE STOPPED PLAY

A swarm of bees had players lying face down during the first Test between Sri Lanka and England at Kandy in 2007.

The ball was hit for six during a Currie Cup match at Paarl in 1995 and landed in a barbecue. Play was halted for 10 minutes while the ball cooled down and the grease was removed.

During an Australia v Pakistan ODI at Trent Bridge in 2001, a Pakistan supporter threw a firework onto the field, prompting the Australian team to walk off.

Burning gravy in the kitchen set off the fire alarm during a county match at Old Trafford in 2007, causing the pavilion to be evacuated.

A bomb scare halted play for 90 minutes at Lord's in 1973 during the Test match against the West Indies.

The gloved Derbyshire wicketkeeper had to remove a prickly hedgehog from the pitch during a county match against Gloucestershire in 1957.

During the Sydney Test against England in 1982–83, a fan released a pig onto the outfield. It was branded 'Botham' on one side and 'Eddie' (Hemmings) on the other.

Start of play on the third day of the India v England Test at Delhi in 1981–82 was delayed when the key to the ball cupboard was mislaid.

Dazzling evening sun forced players from the field at Derby during a day-nighter against Nottinghamshire in 2006.

> At the Oval in 2007 a man dressed in a giant cigarette costume (to promote a smoking ban) strayed behind the bowler's arm. The ensuing delay was finally halted by a PA announcement: 'Would the cigarette please sit down.'

OVER THE LIMIT

Bobby Peel was a key member of the Yorkshire side during the last two decades of the nineteenth century, one of a long line of successful left-arm spinners produced by the county. He gained 20 England caps and toured Australia on four occasions. His 11 for 68 at Old Trafford in 1888 won the Test for England; eight years later at the Oval (his final Test), when Australia were shot out for 44 in their second innings, Peel had figures of 6 for 23.

He also had a drinking problem, in common with many professional cricketers of the time, who often found themselves being treated and toasted by admiring supporters. On one occasion Peel had to be sobered up on the morning of a Test match, though it didn't prevent England winning. Things came to a head in a county match against Middlesex in 1897. Accounts differ as to exactly what took place but, according to teammate George Hirst, Peel was clearly drunk at breakfast. Somehow he made it onto the field and, cap askew, tried to demonstrate to the Yorkshire captain, the disciplinarian Lord Hawke, that he was fit to bowl – but weakened his case by despatching the ball in the wrong direction. He was suspended by the county and never played again. Despite his ignoble exit from the game, Peel remained on good terms with Lord Hawke, who, he said, 'put his arm round me and helped me off the ground – and out of first-class cricket. What a gentleman!'

POLITICALLY INCORRECT

Robin Jackman was called up by England late in his career. The 35-year-old Surrey pace bowler had had an outstanding county season in 1980, for which he was named one of *Wisden*'s Five Cricketers of the Year, and was selected for the side to tour the West Indies that winter. Born in India, where his father was a colonel in the Gurkhas, Jackman had for several years played and coached in South Africa during the English off-season.

England lost the first Test at Port-of-Spain, Trinidad, by an innings and 79 runs. The second match in the series was scheduled to be played at Georgetown, Guyana. The Guyanese government under its dictatorial president Forbes Burnham was strongly opposed to any sporting relations with South Africa (in line with the British Commonwealth's 1977 Gleneagles Agreement) and objected to the presence of Jackman in the England squad. His visa was revoked. Refusing to be dictated to on matters of team selection, the England management cancelled the Test match. There was concern that the other Caribbean nations might follow Guyana's lead, but in the event Barbados, Antigua and Jamaica opted for continuing the series. Jackman made his Test debut at Bridgetown and played in the final match in Jamaica, without conspicuous success. He would play in two more Tests against Pakistan in 1982 before retiring from the game and moving to South Africa, where he became a popular TV cricket commentator.

> ### IT'S A FACT!
> ....
>
> Before their historic ODI against Pakistan at Sharjah in 2012, the Afghanistan cricket team received a 'good luck' message from the Taliban.

FOUL PLAY

One of the most shocking examples of gamesmanship in professional cricket took place in the ODI between Australia and New Zealand at Melbourne in February 1981. It was the third match in the best-of-five final of the Benson & Hedges World Series. Australia, batting first, scored 235 for 4 in their 50 overs, skipper Greg Chappell leading the way with 90. In reply New Zealand had reached 229 for 8 with one ball to go, opener Bruce Edgar still there with 102 to his name.

Facing the final delivery was tail-ender Brian McKechnie, better known as a rugby All Black. Six runs were required to tie the match. The bowler was Trevor Chappell, the third member of the cricketing fraternity. Under instructions from brother Greg, and having consulted with the umpires, Chappell prepared to bowl underarm along the ground, thus making it impossible for the batsman to hit a six. McKechnie blocked the ball at his feet then tossed his bat away in disgust. The New Zealand captain Geoff Howarth ran onto the field to remonstrate with the umpires. In the Benson & Hedges tournament regulations in England underarm bowling was prohibited, but no such rule applied in the Australian competition. The Chappells' tactic was widely condemned, even by their older sibling Ian, who wrote, 'Fair dinkum, Greg, how much pride do you sacrifice to win $35,000?' Richie Benaud described it as 'one of the worst things I have ever seen on a cricket field'. Not long after the incident, the ICC banned underarm bowling in all limited-overs cricket, stating it was 'not within the spirit of the game'.

STRIKE ACTION

In 1976 the South Australian side, led by the abrasive Ian Chappell, went on strike following a dispute over team selection. This was not Chappell's first brush with authority. Earlier in the season he had been censured for breaching the all-white dress code by wearing a pair of clearly branded Adidas boots. The strike, which lasted 18 hours, was called off when the selectors threatened to replace the existing side with an entirely new team. South Australia went on to win the Sheffield Shield, for the second time under Ian Chappell.

UP IN THE AIR

David Gower and Derbyshire batsman John Morris became the centre of controversy during England's 1990–91 tour of Australia. Two down in the series after three Tests, England were playing Queensland at the Carrara Oval on Australia's Gold Coast. The match was a welcome respite from the pressures of Test cricket and for once England, who were batting, were on top – although Gower had been dismissed cheaply. A man with a low boredom threshold, with or without a bat in his hand, Gower had spotted biplanes from a nearby airfield flying over the ground and fancied a flight in one. John Morris, back in the pavilion having scored 132, was eager to join him and together they headed off for a 20-minute flight, calculating that they would be back in time to take to the field should the England innings collapse.

While airborne Gower persuaded the pilot to fly low over the ground, 'buzzing' teammates Robin Smith and Allen Lamb at the crease. The aviators made it back safely to the dressing room but were later confronted by an angry reception committee that included captain Graham Gooch, coach Mickey Stewart and tour manager Peter Lush. The two offenders were treated like recalcitrant schoolboys, creating an atmosphere that did little to improve team morale. Each was fined £1,000, the maximum under the terms of their contracts. There was even talk of sending them home. An unhappy tour ended with Australia winning the series 3–0. It was the beginning of the end for Gower as a Test player, and Morris was never called up by his country again.

FAST AND FURIOUS

The 1979–80 West Indian tour of New Zealand was an ill-tempered affair. The trouble began during the first Test at Dunedin, which the home side narrowly won by one wicket. In New Zealand's second innings an appeal for caught behind was turned down by umpire John Hastie, to which the bowler, Michael Holding, responded by walking down to the striker's end and kicking over the stumps. West Indian captain Clive Lloyd and manager Willie Rodriguez did little to curb the ill feeling, and at the post-match presentations only Desmond Haynes appeared for the tourists, and only then because he had won an award.

The acrimony was carried into the second match at Christchurch, and following another disputed umpiring decision during New Zealand's first innings, the West Indians threatened not to return to the field after the tea interval. Things could hardly have been worse. And yet, on the fourth day fast bowler Colin Croft appealed for a catch behind when Richard Hadlee, on route to a century, was batting. Umpire Fred Goodall turned down the appeal. Croft let rip with a stream of expletives and both umpires spoke to Clive Lloyd, standing unconcerned in the slips. When Croft followed up with a series of bouncers, Goodall no-balled him. The bowler retaliated by flicking off the bails at the bowler's end, and on his approach to the stumps for the next delivery deliberately barged Goodall in the back. Once again Lloyd chose to take no action. The match ended in a draw, as did the final Test in Auckland. Most were glad it was all over.

IT'S A FACT!

In the first Test against Sri Lanka at Pallekelle in 2016, Australia's batsmen faced 154 consecutive deliveries without scoring a run. A new Test record.

CHARACTER STUDIES

❝ *His personality was such that it is remembered by those who played with him to the exclusion of his actual performance.* **❞**

JOHN ARLOTT ON DR W. G. GRACE

ECONOMICAL BOWLER

Bryan 'Bomber' Wells, an off-spinner who played for Gloucestershire and Nottinghamshire in the 1950s and beyond, was the antithesis of the modern professional cricketer. He was considerably overweight and had a less than serious approach to the sport that provided him with a living. He bowled with an almost non-existent run-up – as he put it, two steps when he was cold, one when he was hot and sometimes standing still. Once at Worcester, with the connivance of the batsman, he bowled an entire over while the cathedral clock struck 12. In another county match against Essex, a young batsman kept stepping away from the crease on one pretext or another just before Wells bowled. Bomber embarked on a run around the inner field, returned to his mark, asked the batsman if he was ready and clean bowled him. When he retired in 1965 he had 999 first-class wickets to his name, having declined the chance to make it 1,000 on the grounds that the lesser number was more distinctive. Later, it was discovered that the actual total was only 998. Bomber would have seen the funny side.

CLASSICAL STUMPER

Rev. Archdale Palmer 'Archie' Wickham regularly kept wicket for Somerset between 1891 and 1907. He had a distinctive stance behind the stumps, standing with his head over the bails, legs wide apart, his gloves resting on the top of his pads. He wore a black cummerbund around the waist and his favourite headgear was a Harlequin cap. He would often spout Latin and ancient Greek while he went about his task. For all that, he was an accomplished wicketkeeper and set a world record in a county match against Hampshire at Taunton in 1899 by not conceding a single bye in the county total of 672 for 7. He also has the distinction of being the only cricketer to have played for both sides in a first-class match. In Somerset's fixture against Oxford University in 1901, he kept wicket for the opposition when their own stumper was injured, Wickham himself having already batted. After his death in 1935 his extensive collection of butterflies and moths took up residence in the British Museum.

IT'S A FACT!

The only US president to have watched Test cricket is Dwight D. Eisenhower, who attended the fourth day of the third Test between Pakistan and Australia in 1959. It turned out to be one of the slowest scoring days in Test history!

MELODY MAKER

Left-arm spinner Leslie O'Brien Fleetwood-Smith played ten Tests for Australia in the 1930s, touring England twice. At times almost unplayable, he could also prove very expensive, which limited his appearances at the highest level. With a clipped military-style moustache and a centre parting, Fleetwood-Smith would entertain the crowd with his eccentric behaviour in the outfield. He would sing, whistle (sometimes when bowling), imitate bird calls and practise his golf swing. He was hardly less entertaining with a bat in his hand, though not to his teammates, who were often frustrated by his lack of application. His captain Don Bradman once sent him in to open the innings at the back end of the day on a very sticky wicket. He calculated, correctly, that 'Chuck' wouldn't be good enough to put bat to ball. The next day he made contact for the first time – and was caught out.

YORKSHIRE WIT

Weighing 6.4 kilos (14 lbs 1 oz) at birth, 'Fiery Fred' Trueman was always destined to be a larger-than-life character. One of the greatest fast bowlers the game has seen, he was the first man to take 300 Test wickets and in a career spanning 25 years took 10 or more wickets in a match 25 times, as well as four hat-tricks. There have been countless stories about his gruff Yorkshire humour. When England teammate, Rev. David Sheppard, dropped a catch off his bowling, Fred commented, 'You might keep your eyes shut when you're praying, Rev, but I wish you'd keep 'em open when I'm bowling.' When Raman Subba Row let a ball slip through his hands for four, he apologised to Trueman, saying, 'It might have been better if I'd kept my legs together.' Fred replied, 'Aye, and it's a pity your mother didn't!' He was seldom lost for words. At his daughter's wedding to the son of Raquel Welch, he caught the Hollywood star bending over. 'Gerrup,' he said to her, 'we can see your knickers.'

MEETER 'N' GREETER

The Nottinghamshire opening pair of Walter Keeton and Charlie Harris was one of the best in the county game either side of the Second World War. Unlike his partner, Harris never won an England cap, though he made 360 appearances for his county and scored nearly twenty thousand runs. His humour lifted the spirits of teammates and opponents alike. Going into bat at the start of the day he would habitually greet the fielders with 'Good morning, fellow workers.' Once, when making his entrance from the pavilion in poor light, he carried a torch in one hand and pointedly headed towards square leg instead of the wicket. He upset the rhythm of one established spin bowler by shouting out the type of delivery as the ball left his hand. 'That's the googly,' he would say, or 'That's the leggy' – then played the appropriate shot to show how right he was.

IT'S A FACT!

During the Test between the West Indies and England at Jamaica in 1974, the judge at the nearby high court interrupted proceedings at the trial of a bank robber to read out details of the score.

WHEELER-DEALER

There was something of the Arthur Daly about the Australian Test opener Sid Barnes. He was one of the so-called Invincibles, the all-powerful side that toured England under Don Bradman in 1948. In his 13-Test career, cut short by the war, the New South Welshman averaged an impressive 63.05 with the bat. But, outside cricket, the colourful Barnes was a bit of a wide boy. On the sea voyage to England, while his teammates diligently signed thousands of autographs, he had a rubber stamp made of his own signature and recruited someone on board to do the job for him. In England the tourists were the recipients of dozens of promotional gifts, from cricket equipment to cashmere sweaters. Barnes set up shop in his London hotel bedroom to sell his share to members of the public. On the trip home, with a lot of commercial stock in his luggage, he 'jumped ship' at Melbourne to avoid the more rigorous customs scrutiny at Sydney, making the last leg of the journey by train. The dodge worked.

CRICKETERS ON CRICKETERS

'A dour, remorseless Scot, a hundred and thirty years after his time. He should have gone to Australia in charge of a convict hulk.'
Australian opener Jack Fingleton on England 'bodyline' captain Douglas Jardine

'I have seen God. He bats at no. 4 for India in Tests.'
Matthew Hayden on Sachin Tendulkar

'He was all bristle and bullshit and I couldn't make out what he was saying, except that every sledge ended with "arsewipe".'
Mike Atherton on Australian fast bowler Merv Hughes

'I love watching Virat Kohli bat. He reminds me of myself.'
Sir Viv Richards

'Bradman was a team in himself. I think the Don was too good: he spoilt the game… I do not think we want to see another one quite like him. I do not think we ever shall.'
Sir Jack Hobbs on Sir Donald Bradman

'I guess some guys are just naturally built for comfort rather than cricket.'
Bob Willis on Rob Key

> 'The face of a choirboy, the demeanour of a civil
> servant and the ruthlessness of a rat-catcher.'
> **Geoffrey Boycott on England spinner**
> **Derek Underwood**

> 'Denis Compton was the only player to call his partner for a
> run and wish him good luck at the same time.'
> **Middlesex teammate John Warr**

> 'Off the field he could be your lifelong buddy, but out in the middle
> he had all the loveable qualities of a demented rhinoceros.'
> **Colin McCool on fellow Australian leg-spinner Bill O'Reilly**

> 'A natural mistimer of the ball.'
> **Angus Fraser on Mike Atherton**

CHEEKY CHAPPIE

Nicknamed 'Arkle' (after the steeplechaser, who was also fast over the turf), the Nottinghamshire batsman Derek Randall was one of the liveliest characters in cricket. He scored seven centuries in his 47 Test appearances and saved almost as many runs with his brilliant fielding, mainly in the covers. At the crease, he was constantly fidgeting and full of chat. In the Centenary Test at Melbourne in 1976, with England trying to chase down a target of 463 to win, Randall stood alone with a magnificent innings of 174. Goaded by his physical jerks and perky attitude (and the runs he was piling up), an exasperated Dennis Lillee sent down a savage bouncer. The batsman ducked out of harm's way, then doffed his cap and quipped, 'No point hitting me there, mate, there's nothing in it.' He left the field to a standing ovation but by the wrong gate and found himself heading for the royal enclosure, from where the Queen was watching the game. It was pure Randall.

FRIENDLY ARBITRATOR

The former Leicestershire fast bowler Alec Skelding became one of England's most popular umpires. Throughout his playing days he wore spectacles. Asked once if he found them a hindrance, he said: 'I can't see without 'em and on hot days I can't see with 'em, because they get steamed up. So I bowl on hearing only and appeal twice an over.' As an umpire he once responded to an appeal for a run-out with the observation, 'That was a "photo-finish" and as there isn't time to develop the plate, I shall say not out.' He would cheerfully be the butt of other people's humour. In a match against the 1948 Australians, he turned down a vigorous appeal by the tourists. Shortly after, a small dog ran onto the playing area and was picked up by Sid Barnes. He carried it over to Skelding with the words, 'Here you are. All you want now is a white stick!'

IT'S A FACT!

The West Indian batsman Lawrence Rowe, who uniquely scored a double and single hundred on Test debut in 1972, was allergic to grass!

COMIC TURN

Johnny Wardle, the Yorkshire left-arm spinner, was a natural comedian, but as with many funny men there was a darker side. His career coincided with that of the Surrey left-armer Tony Lock, who was often chosen ahead of Wardle to represent England – though many pundits believed the Yorkshireman to be the better bowler. As it was, he took 102 wickets in his 28 Tests (at an average of 20) but felt he was a victim of the North–South divide. On the field he liked to clown, a favourite trick being to throw the ball over his head and catch it behind his back. He once took a very smart catch off his own bowling, but pretending that the ball had actually passed him, had Fred Trueman haring off towards the boundary, only to realise he was chasing nothing. Wardle then laughingly produced the ball from his pocket. In New Zealand, during the MCC tour of 1954–55, he was next man in and walked to the wicket carrying a giant-sized bat. Anything for a laugh!

HILLSIDE HECKLER

Real name Stephen Harold Gascoigne (1878–1942), 'Yabba' was cricket's most famous barracker. He could be found on the Hill at the Sydney Cricket Ground on most match days, gearing up for some more memorable one-liners. When a becalmed batsman at last scored, Yabba yelled, 'Whoa there! He's bolted.' To a bowler whose sense of direction had gone astray, he shouted, 'Your length is lousy but you bowl a good width.' He had a loud voice, instantly recognisable to most in the crowd and many of the players. Very knowledgeable about the game, he never resorted to vulgarity or abuse, and unlike many of those around him normally restricted himself to two bottles of beer a day. On one occasion an umpire was standing in the middle with his hand raised, directing one of the ground staff to move the sightscreen. 'It's no use, Umpire,' called out Yabba, 'you'll have to wait till playtime like the rest of us.'

SUPERSTITIONS

Playing a sport in which luck has such a large role, it's no wonder that many cricketers are superstitious. Some have their lucky seat in the dressing room or on the team bus, while others put on their gear in a particular order; among Indian cricketers, Sachin Tendulkar always attached his left pad first, Rahul Dravid his right – either way it seemed to work.

Another Indian batsman, Virender Sehwag, on the advice of his numerologist, opted for a numberless shirt in order to engender good fortune at the crease. His teammate Sourav Ganguly always carried a photograph of his guru in the pocket of his flannels. For years, Australia's Steve Waugh kept a red rag in his pocket when batting – a superstitious habit that stemmed from the Headingley Test in 1993, when Waugh scored a century and used the same rag to mop sweat from his brow.

Two of England's greatest post-war batsmen preferred not to rely entirely on their skills when at the crease. Denis Compton had a silver four-leaf clover to bring him luck, and Len Hutton a five-shilling coin. Virat Kohli finds his *kada*, a lucky charm, does the trick.

South African speed merchant Dale Steyn makes a point of stepping onto the field left foot first, while for his Australian counterpart Brett Lee it was always a matter of putting on his left boot ahead of the right.

But when it comes to superstitious rituals the former Hampshire and South African batsman Neil McKenzie is in a league of his own. He would routinely tape his bat to the dressing room ceiling for good luck, and before heading to the wicket he would ensure that all the toilet seat lids were lowered. An added insurance was to get out of bed three times before every game. How unlucky is that!

MATCH WINNERS

....

Stop whatever you're doing and turn on the England–Ireland match.
SOUTH AFRICA'S AB DE VILLIERS (ON TWITTER, 2011)

Cricket, of course, is a team game, but every so often the symbolic victory garland belongs around the neck of an individual player without whose truly exceptional performance in the match it might have been a different story.

OLD TRAFFORD, 1956

England and Australia met for the fourth Test with the five-match series standing at 1–1. A victory for England would retain them the Ashes. The home side, batting first, scored 459, with centuries from Colin Cowdrey and Rev. David Sheppard, who was playing his first Test since taking up holy orders. Australia began their reply 45 minutes after lunch on the second day, and after an opening stand of 48 were all out for 84 – Jim Laker 9 for 37. In his spell after tea the Surrey off-spinner took 7 for 8 in 22 balls. Rain restricted play on Saturday and most of Monday

(Sunday being a rest day), and Australia began the final day on 84 for 2. Laker and his county spinning partner Tony Lock, who had taken the only other wicket in the first innings, continued the attack on a pitch that was showing signs of breaking up. One by one the Australian batsmen were despatched, with even the great Neil Harvey bagging a pair. At 5.27 p.m. the tenth wicket fell, all of them to Jim Laker, who finished with match figures of 19 for 90. (All his wickets had been taken from the Stretford End.) Even in a game as unpredictable as cricket, his performance is unlikely to be equalled. As for the Australians, it was déjà vu. In their match against Surrey two months earlier their nemesis had taken 10 for 88 in the first innings. No wonder they call it 'Laker's Year'!

IT'S A FACT!

Playing for Nepal against Mozambique in a World Cup League Division Five game in Jersey in 2008, Mahaboob Alam took all ten wickets for 12 runs. A world record for any limited-overs international.

LORD'S, 1972

Bob Massie, a right-arm medium-fast bowler from Western Australia, was largely unknown to English fans when he made his debut in the second Test at Lord's. All that was about to change. The 25-year-old opened the bowling with Dennis

Lillee, England having won the toss and elected to bat. The humid conditions favoured Massie's swing more than Lillee's pace. Bowling round the wicket, the debutant moved the ball sharply in both directions, troubling all the England batsmen. The home side were all out for 272, with Massie taking 8 for 84 in 32.5 overs. Thanks to England's own fast bowler John Snow (5 for 57), Australia's lead was restricted to 36. Then it was Massie's turn again. Taking up where he had left off, he gave an almost repeat performance as England were shot out for 116 – Massie 8 for 53. Until the Indian spinner Narendra Hirwani shaved Massie's record by one run in 1988, the Australian's match figures of 16 for 137 were a record for a bowler on their Test debut. But almost as suddenly as he had burst onto the Test scene, Massie vacated it. He took just 15 wickets in his remaining five Tests, his ability to swing the ball both ways at will deserting him. Within a couple of years his first-class career was over and he returned to relative obscurity.

PERMANENTLY CAST

The first cricketer to be commemorated with a statue was K. S. 'Ranji' Ranjitsinhji, whose sculpted likeness was erected in Jamnagar in the 1930s. Australia boasts four statues of Sir Donald Bradman, including one at the Melbourne Cricket Ground. W. G. Grace can be seen at Lord's, Fred Trueman in his home town of Skipton, Harold Larwood at Kirby-in-Ashfield in Nottinghamshire and

Essex boy Graham Gooch in Chelmsford. Dickie Bird has his finger permanently aloft in Barnsley, the first umpire to be honoured in this fashion. Bronze replicas of Brian Lara (Port-of-Spain) and Sir Viv Richards (Antigua) are among the statuary tributes to great West Indian cricketers, the most imposing of which is the monument to the Three Ws (Weekes, Worrell and Walcott) in Barbados. The achievements of Sachin Tendulkar are uniquely celebrated in Mumbai with a giant steel 'Bat of Honour' that is over 7.5 m (25 ft) high and weighs 2 tonnes.

BOMBAY, 1980

India and England met at Bombay (now Mumbai) for the one-off Golden Jubilee Test, celebrating 50 years of the host nation's cricketing Board of Control. But in all other respects it was 'Botham's Test'. Having won the toss, India batted first in overcast conditions on an uncharacteristically grassy pitch that gave some help to the bowlers. Skilfully exploiting the conditions (and aided and abetted by Derbyshire's Bob Taylor, who took seven catches behind the stumps), Ian Botham was the main wicket-taker with 6 for 58 as India were all out for 242. At 58 for 5 England looked in even worse shape, but a commanding innings of 114 from the Somerset all-rounder gave the visitors a useful lead of 54. In a golden moment of sportsmanship, the Indian captain Gundappa Viswanath summoned Bob Taylor – Botham's principal support with the bat as well as the ball – back to the wicket after the umpire had erroneously given him out, caught behind off Kapil Dev. Together they put on a pivotal 171 for the sixth wicket. Back with ball in hand, England's one-man band was ready for his next solo. Taking 7 for 48 (three more catches for Taylor, whose ten for the match was a world record), Botham scuppered India for 149 in the second innings. Needing only 96 to win, it was England's match by ten wickets. Ian Botham became the first male cricketer to score a century and take ten wickets in the same Test (Australia's Betty Wilson had performed the feat in 1958).

LAHORE, 1996

Australia were favourites to win the sixth ICC World Cup final. Their opponents, Sri Lanka, had never made it this far before, whereas for Australia it was third time around and they had had the experience of winning the Cup in 1987. Led by Mark Taylor, they fielded a strong side. The batting line-up included Ricky Ponting, Mark and Steve Waugh and the world's most accomplished 'finisher', Michael Bevan. Among the bowlers were Shane Warne and Glenn McGrath. Sri Lanka's captain Arjuna Ranatunga won the toss and put Australia in to bat. Taylor led the way with 74 and there were useful contributions from Ponting and Bevan. Given the strength of the Australian bowling attack, their total of 241 for 7 seemed just about enough, even more so when Sri Lanka found themselves at 23 for 2, their star batsman Sanath Jayasuriya already back in the pavilion. Aravinda de Silva joined Asanka Gurusinha and together they put on 125 before the latter was bowled by Paul Reiffel. It was the last Sri Lankan wicket to fall. De Silva, in an exhilarating display that saw the ball despatched to all parts of the ground, scored 107 off 124 balls. Sri Lanka were home with nearly four overs to spare, and de Silva, who also took three wickets and two catches, was sole contender for Man of the Match.

IT'S A FACT!

England's score of 444 for 3 against Pakistan at Trent Bridge in 2016 was the highest total ever recorded in an ODI. Their 59 boundaries, including 16 sixes, was another world record. In the final 30 overs of their innings, England averaged a boundary every four deliveries.

BANGALORE, 2011

For England, the match against Ireland in the group stage of the 2011 World Cup seemed little more than a formality. The bookmakers agreed, at one stage offering odds of 400–1 on an Irish victory. Batting first, England made 327 for 8, Jonathan Trott (92) and Ian Bell (81) the top scorers. Some tight bowling at the death restricted England to 15 runs in the last three overs, but at the halfway mark few gave Ireland any chance at all. They began their innings disastrously, with captain William Porterfield chopping the very first ball (from Jimmy Anderson) onto his stumps. After a solid recovery the wickets began to tumble, the third falling at 103, the fifth at 111. Enter Kevin O'Brien, whose regular team was the Railway Union Cricket

Club in Dublin and whose older brother Niall, like their father Brendan before them, also played for Ireland. The 26-year-old all-rounder, who had never made a 50 in nine previous World Cup innings, took the England attack apart. His innings of 113 came off 63 balls, with 6 sixes and 13 fours. Dropped on 91 by Andrew Strauss, he reached his century in 50 balls – the fastest in World Cup history and 16 deliveries fewer than it took the previous record holder Matthew Hayden. O'Brien was run out in the penultimate over, but Ireland didn't falter, winning the match by three wickets with five balls remaining. It was much more than just the luck of the Irish.

VERITABLE WICKET-TAKER

In a County Championship game against Nottinghamshire at Headingley in 1932, the Yorkshire left-arm spinner Hedley Verity took 10 for 10 in the visitors' second innings. At one stage he captured seven wickets in 15 balls, including a hat-trick (in all he bowled 19.4 overs, 16 of them maidens). It remains the best bowling analysis in first-class cricket. Seven years later at Hove, on the last day of county cricket before the outbreak of the Second World War, he was at it again. His 7 for 9 in six overs saw Sussex shot out for 33 and sealed Yorkshire's victory, Verity taking a wicket with his final ball in first-class cricket. A captain in the Green Howards during the war, the Yorkshireman died in an Italian POW camp from wounds received on the battlefield. His grave is at Caserta in southern Italy.

AROUND THE GROUNDS

....

❝ *Lord's! What tender recollections*
Does that famous name suggest! ❞
FROM 'LORD'S' BY HARRY GRAHAM (1874–1936)

The Melbourne Cricket Ground (known to locals as 'The G') is the world's largest. It has a seating capacity close to 100,000 and plays host to Australian-rules football as well as cricket. Eden Gardens, home to the Indian Premier League's Kolkata Knight Riders, comes second with a normal capacity of 66,000, though it has been known to pack in thousands more. England's biggest venue, Lord's, which currently holds a maximum of 30,000, is way down the list. In fact, among Test-playing nations, only the West Indies and Zimbabwe rank lower in terms of the size of their largest stadium.

It was the Oval, in 1880, which staged the first ever Test match in England. Lord's didn't get a look-in until four years later, by which time England and Australia had chalked up 14 Tests against each other. The honour of hosting the first ODI in England, against Australia in 1972, went to Old Trafford. Australia were once again the opponents for the inaugural

Twenty20 international on home soil, at the Rose Bowl in 2005. For the record, England were the winners in all three formats.

> ### IT'S A FACT!
>
> During a solo 8,000-mile (12,900-km) cricket tour through Eastern Europe in 2006, Scotsman Angus Bell hit a ball from one side of the Bosphorus to the other – from Europe to Asia, right over the boundary.

WHAT'S IN A NAME?

One of Australia's most famous Test grounds is 'The Gabba' – shortened from Woolloongabba, the suburb of Brisbane in which it is located. Across the other side of the continent, in Perth, is the Western Australian Cricket Association (WACA), best known for the pace and bounce of its pitch and for the Freemantle Doctor, the cooling afternoon breeze that blows in from the sea.

New Zealand's oldest ground of any note is the Basin Reserve in Wellington, commonly referred to as 'The Basin'. Nearby is the newer Westpac Stadium, which during the winter months is home to the Hurricanes Super Rugby team. A multi-purpose facility which stages ODIs and Twenty20 games, its shape and structure have earned it the nickname 'The Cake Tin'. Johannesburg's Wanderers Stadium is the city's third Test venue, following the original Wanderers ground and Ellis Park, more familiar to rugby fans. Visiting players have christened it 'The Bull Ring' on account of its intimidating atmosphere.

Two grounds that sound confusingly alike but could hardly be more different are the Kennington Oval in London and the Kensington Oval in Bridgetown, Barbados. Only one of them has a gasometer as a landmark.

IT'S A FACT!

St Lucia renamed its Test ground the Darren Sammy National Cricket Stadium, after the man who led the West Indies to victory in the 2016 ICC World Twenty20.

VANISHING GROUNDS

Cricket grounds, like everything else to do with the game, are subject to change. Some have been redeveloped almost beyond recognition. New stands have been built over the carcasses of the old, open spaces have been enclosed, hospitality suites have put on weight. Commemorative names have come and gone, as have the distracting logos of sponsors. Some first-class grounds have disappeared altogether. Priory Meadow in Hastings, one of Sussex's seaside grounds and the venue for an annual end-of-season Cricket Week, is no more. Neither is Hampshire's former county ground at Southampton, its role usurped by the Rose Bowl. Bramall Lane, Sheffield, which staged a Test match in 1902, is now a modern football stadium.

MISSING LANDMARKS

Some landmarks have also dropped out of sight, though not always as the price of development. Parr's Tree at Trent Bridge was a long-standing elm, until blown down by a gale in 1976. It was named after George Parr, an outstanding cricketer of the mid-nineteenth century, who for nearly 30 years struck the ball over, past and through the tree on the edge of the boundary. Some of the salvaged wood was used to make commemorative coffee tables and over 2,000 miniature cricket bats.

Another tree that fell victim to strong winds was the famous lime at the St Lawrence Ground at Canterbury, Kent's headquarters. The 200-year-old tree stood, uniquely, inside the boundary. Shots blocked by its substantial presence counted as four, anything over the top was six – a rare feat, last accomplished by the West Indian all-rounder Carl Hooper.

For decades, the Hill at the Sydney Cricket Ground, a grassy mound where spectators sat and watched and drank beer, had been the haunt of barrackers. More sensitive players hated the prospect of having to field within earshot of their ribald comments and, occasionally, within range of their missiles. In 2007, it gave way to the 12,000-seater Victor Trumper Stand.

The Old Tavern pub at Lord's was opened in 1868 and survived long enough to celebrate its centenary – but only just. In 1968 the New Tavern Stand went up in its place and the call 'Time, gentlemen, please' became a faint memory. A group of cricket-loving actors and broadcasters who used to gather at the old bar to watch the cricket were, in 1950, inspired to form a charity in its name. They called it the Lord's Taverners.

CRICKET UNDERGROUND

Cricket matches have been played in Antarctica, up Mt Everest and on the volcanic ash of Ascension Island in the South Atlantic, but in Cumbria in 2013 they staged the first ever fixture underground. The venue was the Honister slate mine and the game was between the villages of Caldbeck and Threlkeld, a fundraiser for the latter, whose cricket pitch had been recently flooded. The match took place in a floodlit cavern 600 m (2,000 ft) below ground, the players wearing hard hats. There were six overs per innings, each bowler restricted to one over. No boundaries meant that the batsmen had to leg it for every run. Caldbeck emerged into the light victorious.

SPECTACULAR SIGHTS

There are some grounds around the world where the action on the field has to compete with the eye-catching attractions off it.

The Newlands stadium at Cape Town, scene of many a Test match, has the contrasting contours of Table Mountain, Devil's Peak and Signal Hill as a permanent backdrop. Jamaica's Sabina Park is overlooked by the Blue Mountains, home of the coffee that bears its name. The Queenstown Cricket Ground in New Zealand's South Island, which staged its first ODI in 2003, sits in the shadow of the aptly named Remarkables. But the prize for the most spectacular mountain scenery on view must surely go to the HPCA Stadium at Dharamsala in India, where the towering snow-capped Himalayas oversee the summer game.

The Arnos Vale ground on the island of St Vincent lies within a cricket ball's throw of the Caribbean. Pukekura Park in New Plymouth, arguably New Zealand's most beautiful cricket ground, is surrounded by native bush and natural lakes, with Mt Taranaki in the distance.

Historic buildings are more of a feature around England's county venues. Looming over the Riverside ground at Chester-le-Street is the fourteenth-century Lumley Castle. Spectators at Chesterfield's Queen's Park can look up at the famous crooked spire of St Mary and All Saints Church. At Worcester it is the magnificent cathedral that dominates the skyline, with the River Severn alongside – a mixed blessing for the New Road ground, which has often been flooded. At Arundel, the picturesque cricket field is in the grounds of the castle itself; confusingly, especially to visitors from overseas, Arundel is the seat of the Duke of Norfolk, though located firmly in Sussex, whose county side plays there.

IT'S A FACT!

Cricketers playing in a tournament in the Queensland outback in 1998 killed a number of pythons and a highly venomous Taipan snake while searching for lost balls.

TEST GROUNDS IN ENGLAND AND WALES*

EDGBASTON (BIRMINGHAM)

Capacity: 25,000
Built: 1882
First Test: 1902 (England v Australia)
Fact: In 2004, England's Marcus Trescothick became the first batsman to score a hundred in each innings of an Edgbaston Test (v West Indies).

TRENT BRIDGE (NOTTINGHAM)

Capacity: 17,500
Built: 1841
First Test: 1899 (England v Australia)
Fact: On the opening day of the 2015 Test against Australia, the tourists were dismissed for 60 in 111 balls – the shortest first innings in Test history.

SWALEC STADIUM (CARDIFF)

Capacity: 16,000
Built: 2008
First Test: 2009 (England v Australia)
Fact: Formerly Sophia Gardens, home of Glamorganshire County Cricket Club since 1967.

LORD'S (LONDON)

Capacity: 30,000
Built: 1814
First Test: 1884 (England v Australia)
Fact: The playing area drops 2.5 m (8 ft) from north to south: the famous Lord's slope.

THE OVAL (LONDON)

Capacity: 23,500
Built: 1845
First Test: 1880 (England v Australia)
Fact: The Oval ground was laid with 10,000 grass turfs transplanted from Tooting Common.

ROSE BOWL (SOUTHAMPTON)

Capacity: 15,000
Built: 2001
First Test: 2011 (England v Sri Lanka)
Fact: In 2013, Australia's Aaron Finch set a new world record for Twenty20 internationals by scoring 156 runs off 63 balls (v England).

OLD TRAFFORD (MANCHESTER)

Capacity: 26,000
Built: 1857
First Test: 1884 (England v Australia)
Fact: In the Ashes Test of 1993, Shane Warne dismissed Mike Gatting with what has been called the 'ball of the century'.

RIVERSIDE GROUND (CHESTER-LE-STREET)

Capacity: 17,000
Built: 1995
First Test: 2003 (England v Zimbabwe)
Fact: The Riverside was the first new Test venue in England since 1902.

HEADINGLEY (LEEDS)

Capacity: 20,000
Built: 1890
First Test: 1899 (England v Australia)
Fact: Bob Willis's 8 for 43 against Australia in 1981 remains the best Test bowling analysis at the ground.

* Bramall Lane in Sheffield, built in 1855 and used as a ground by Yorkshire until 1973, staged one Test match (v Australia) in 1902.

THE FLIP SIDE

> *Cricket is indescribable. How do you describe an orgasm?*
> **GREG MATTHEWS, AUSTRALIAN ALL-ROUNDER**

Cricket when played seriously is no laughing matter, except perhaps to those who don't understand it. But it is by and large a good-humoured game, one that has often attracted eccentric characters – on and off the field – and cultivated the bizarre. No other sport delights so much in its oddities.

CRICKET AT SEA

Few cricket matches are over as quickly as the annual Bramble Bank fixture. Staged once a year on a sandbank in the middle of the Solent – usually in late August or early September at low tide, when the venue briefly surfaces – the game generally lasts no more than an hour, after which the sea reasserts itself. Teams, and their supporters, from the Royal Southern Yacht Club at Hamble and the Island Sailing Club on the Isle of Wight arrive at the 'ground' in a flotilla of boats, the players wearing full cricket regalia.

Speed is of the essence. Depending on how much the sea has receded, batsmen and bowlers can be above their ankles in water, with fieldsmen in the deep just that. It's not the winning that's important but the taking part. There isn't time for a tea interval – after all, who wants soggy sandwiches? – just a big slap-up dinner when everyone has dried off.

SOME OF CRICKET'S MOST UNUSUAL NAMES

Julius Caesar
Played for Surrey in the mid-nineteenth century. A batsman and brilliant outfielder, he went on the first overseas tours to North America and Australia.

Sachin Baby
Named by his cricket-mad father after Sachin Tendulkar, Baby has played as a middle-order batsman in the Indian Premier League and for the India A cricket team.

Richard Chee Quee
Right-hand batsman for New South Wales in the 1990s, he was the first cricketer of Chinese origin to play at first-class level in Australia.

Napoleon Einstein
Played for the India Under-19s and for the Chennai Super Kings, then became a break dancer.

Xenophon Balaskas

Of Greek stock, Balaskas was a leg-spinner and useful lower-order batsman who played nine Tests for South Africa in the 1930s.

Sidney Kitcat

An all-rounder, he regularly turned out for Gloucestershire in the 1890s and early 1900s.

Pikky Ya France

Middle-order batsman and occasional slow bowler who plays first-class cricket in Namibia.

John and Roger Human

The Human brothers, both all-rounders, played English county cricket in the 1930s, John for Middlesex, Roger for Worcestershire.

WIDE OF THE MARK

In a Minor Counties fixture between Dorset and Cheshire in 1988, the Dorset captain contrived to set up an interesting finish to the game by conceding quick runs. He instructed his bowler to send down a series of very wide wides, each of which would go to the boundary. Fourteen wides were bowled in the over and four runs were scored off the bat. Sixty runs in all. Given a fighting chance of victory, Cheshire took up the challenge but lost the match by 18 runs.

LOOK-A-LIKES

Former Australian wicketkeeper Ian Healy is a skilful impersonator of famous bowling actions. In a testimonial match for Allan Border in 1993, he imitated fellow Australian pace men Terry Alderman and Merv Hughes (complete with padded stomach and false moustache), West Indian speedster Malcolm Marshall and Pakistani leg-spinner Abdul Qadir all in one over. In the guise of Malcolm Marshall, he clean bowled the latter's former teammate Joel Garner. The original couldn't have done it better.

ARMCHAIR CRICKETER

David Harris was one of England's most formidable cricketers during the last quarter of the eighteenth century. Bowling underarm, he generated real pace and could make the ball lift sharply off a length. Many a batsman had his unprotected fingers painfully crushed against the bat handle. Towards the end of his career, Harris, a Hampshire professional, suffered from gout. Stoically refusing to give up the game he loved – and was so good at – he frequently supported himself on a crutch when bowling. On really bad days he would sit out alternate overs in an armchair, positioned at a safe distance behind the wicket.

> ## IT'S A FACT!
>
> Martin McGuinness, the Sein Fein politician and former commander in the IRA, became hooked on cricket as a teenager in the late 1960s and has been an avid fan ever since.

ELEVEN AGAINST TWO

In 1936, two professional cricketers took on an entire XI from the Isle of Oxney in a charity match at Wittersham in Kent. The occasion marked a similar contest a century before in which two Kent pros had defeated the home side, a result the Oxney men were now hoping to reverse.

The professional pair this time around was the Kent opening batsman Bill Ashdown (the only cricketer whose first-class career began before the First World War and lasted until after the Second) and the Sussex all-rounder Bert Wensley. The two men rotated the bowling and wicketkeeping duties and shared the fielding. The Isle of Oxney XI batted first and were all out for 153, a total which the two-man opposition overhauled without losing a wicket – leaving the Isle of Oxney all to do in 2036.

TOURIST ATTRACTION

The Australian Aboriginal team that toured England in 1868 was the first overseas side to do so. During their five-month tour, the 13-man side played a total of 47 matches (14 wins, 14 defeats, 19 draws) kitted out in a distinctively patriotic uniform of red shirt, blue sash and white flannels. Their native names being beyond the grasp of the British public, most of the players were known by nicknames. When they were not engaged in playing cricket, Dick-a-Dick, Bullocky, Mosquito, Jim Crow, Twopenny and others demonstrated their skills with boomerang and spear in front of enthusiastic crowds. Sadly, one of the party, King Cole, never made it home, dying of tuberculosis in a London hospital.

IT'S A FACT!

The first overseas tour by an English side was to have been to Paris in August 1789, but for once it wasn't rain that stopped play but the French Revolution.

SMOKERS V NON-SMOKERS

In 1887, a four-day match took place in Melbourne between adherents of the noxious weed and those who managed to live without it. The two sides were made up of members of Alfred Shaw's England XI, at the time touring Australia, and cricketers from the host country. Batting first, the Non-Smokers amassed a healthy 803, the highest total hitherto recorded in a first-class game, with England batsman Arthur Shrewsbury scoring 236. Despite the presence of several England players in their own line-up, the Smokers could only manage 356 and were forced to follow on. They were 135 for 5 in their second innings when the match finally ran out of puff.

EXTRA RUNS

The Surrey and England fast bowler Alf Gover was a member of Lord Tennyson's side that toured India in 1937–38. During the tour several players succumbed to dysentery (the so-called Delhi belly), and one day it was Gover's turn. He had just started his run-up when the tell-tale stomach cramps gripped him. Without breaking his stride, and still clutching the ball, he continued to run – past the umpire, past the batsman at the crease, past the wicketkeeper standing back – straight on into the pavilion. As he told the story later, he was two yards too late.

FAMILY AFFAIR

For the first and only time in county cricket, a father and son batted together against a father-and-son bowling attack. This unique event took place on the second day of the match between Derbyshire and Warwickshire in June 1922. Warwickshire's Willie Quaife and his son Bernard were in partnership at the crease, facing the home side's bowling attack of Billy Bestwick and his son Robert. Bernard Quaife was dismissed for 20 but his father went on to score 107 (before being bowled by Robert Bestwick). It was a good day for both families, with the Bestwicks sharing six wickets between them.

UMPIRE'S DECISION

In 1948, Glamorgan won the County Championship for the first time in the club's history. The Welsh side had been a late starter, not achieving first-class status until 1921, the 17th county to do so. Their Championship moment of glory came on the third day of the match against Hampshire at Bournemouth. Having completely dominated the game throughout, Glamorgan had just one more wicket to take. The last Hampshire batsman was rapped on the pads and the umpire, former Glamorgan player Dai Davies, raised his finger and shouted, 'You're out – and we've won!'

CRICKET IN THE SADDLE

The following advertisement appeared in the *Kentish Gazette* on 29 April 1794:

Cricketing on Horseback. A very singular game of cricket will be played on Tuesday the 6th of May in

Linstead Park between the Gentlemen of the Hill and the Gentlemen of the Dale, for one guinea a man. The whole to be performed on horseback. To begin at 9 o'clock, and the game to be played out. A good ordinary [meal] on the ground by John Hogben.

THE CHANGING GAME

❝ *One-day cricket is an exhibition.*
Test cricket is an examination. **❞**
HENRY BLOFELD, CRICKET WRITER AND COMMENTATOR

Over the 300 years of its recorded history, cricket has shown itself to be a resilient and adaptable sport, and one that continues to attract new adherents. In addition to the ten Test-playing nations, there are currently 39 ICC associate members – Saudi Arabia is the latest recruit – and, spanning the globe, a further 56 affiliate members. Who knows, if the spirit of cricket is allowed to prevail there might be hope for the world after all.

But despite the game's missionary spread, its future direction at the professional level is far from clear. Since the inaugural match in Melbourne in 1877, Test cricket has been universally recognised as the pre-eminent expression of the sport and for players the ultimate accolade. However, Ashes series aside and with England in general the honourable exception, crowds at Test matches are declining. Television coverage in South Africa, India, New Zealand, Sri Lanka and the Caribbean regularly displays a backdrop of woefully empty stands. In brazenly sharp contrast, the Indian Premier League and Australia's Big Bash play their Twenty20 fixtures in front of packed houses.

The financial balance of power, along with the spectators, is shifting from Test cricket to the shorter format – the new kid on the block – and with it political muscle within the ICC. There are fears of a serious rift developing as the richer countries push for a greater say in the running of the game. Words like 'brand', 'product' and 'merchandise' have become part of cricket's vocabulary.

Most commentators would agree that there is too much Test cricket being played (indeed too much cricket of any sort). The gulf between the strongest and weakest sides has prompted plans to divide the ten Test countries (with the addition of the two strongest non-Test nations to boost numbers) into two leagues, with promotion and relegation, broadly along the lines of English county cricket. But it hasn't been plain sailing. Since the ICC consists of representatives of the national cricket boards, opposition to a two-tier structure that would inevitably diminish those banished to the lower league has been fierce in some quarters.

England, Australia, South Africa and India – despite the latter's puzzlingly poor record away from home – remain the most consistently successful sides. Among the others, Bangladesh and Zimbabwe struggle to make significant progress at Test level (though the former's first ever victory against England in 2016 has given cricket in Bangladesh a healthy boost); the glory days of the West Indies have become a distant memory; and with little sign of security returning to their homeland any time soon, the nomadic Pakistan team has been forced to pitch its tent in the United Arab Emirates, though they still continue to be a formidable side.

NEW INITIATIVES

The impact of Twenty20 cricket has been as great on the field as off. Improvisation is the name of the game, with players adapting their tactics and techniques to achieve success, often with spectacular results. This brash addition to cricket's repertoire has inevitably caught the imagination of younger fans, their enthusiasm undented by the monotonous choreography of the dancing girls at the boundary edge. If the cash-rich leagues continue to prosper, the next generation of young cricketers could well make Twenty20 their principal focus.

Lacking the gravitas of Test cricket or the flair of Twenty20, the 50-overs game sometimes appears old hat, not least during the stuttering early stages of the four-yearly World Cup. Routinely tacked onto either end of a Test series, the fixtures are like guests who turn up to a party too soon or linger long after it is all over. If the international load needs to be lightened – and it does – the administrators could begin by culling the ubiquitous ODI.

In 2016, the ECB introduced a points system across all three formats for the two summer tours, along the lines of that adopted in the women's game. This initiative, it is hoped, will help sustain interest in a tour beyond the Test series, though traditionalists may find it hard to swallow when (or if) it comes to the Ashes.

On the domestic front, county cricket has been restructured once again, but fundamental problems remain. With the country's top players contracted to the ECB, and others lining their pockets in the Indian Premier League, the counties have been forced to call on the services of overseas mercenaries, who make their exits and entrances with bewildering speed. The four-day game, the breeding ground for England's Test cricketers, is increasingly under threat, largely unwatched and heavily subsidised.

Currently, all domestic competitions, whatever the format, involve the 18 first-class counties. But that could soon change. The ECB has advanced plans to introduce a new Twenty20 tournament that would feature just eight 'super' teams, based in major cities or regions. The aim is to attract the world's top players, boost crowds and increase revenue. Australia's highly successful Big Bash is the working model. It will, however, inevitably mean many of the existing counties missing out.

Despite the undoubted advances in women's cricket, mixed teams seem a distant prospect, except perhaps for certain one-off fixtures such as benefit matches. Staging Twenty20 double-headers, with men's and women's games played back to back, could increase attendance figures and give the female franchise greater exposure.

The game's administrators and pundits will doubtless continue to ponder these and other problems, to good or bad effect. Happily, whatever the decisions of the powers that be, cricket at the grass roots will remain largely undisturbed. On village greens and in urban parks, on close-cut playing fields and in sheep-shorn meadows, and wherever else cricketers of all ages can cheerfully engage with bat and ball, there will be nothing more at stake than the inherent delight of the summer game itself.

10 WAYS IN WHICH THE GAME HAS CHANGED IN RECENT YEARS

- The excessive celebrations on reaching a three-figure score, including jumping in the air, running down the pitch, kissing the helmet badge and sometimes the ground.

- Batsmen touching gloves between overs or after a boundary.

- The fielding side going into a huddle only moments after leaving the dressing room.

- Positioning sunglasses on the back of headgear.

- Batsmen no longer walking to the wicket side by side at the start of a new session.

- Bowlers holding the ball aloft after a five-wicket haul.

- Batsmen not accepting the fielder's word that a catch has been a fair one.

- Players shouting encouragement to each other from all parts of the field.

- Retrospective checks that a bowler hasn't overstepped the mark before giving a batsman out.

- Dutifully wearing the sponsor's cap when giving media interviews.

THE LANGUAGE
OF CRICKET

· ·

The origins of some of cricket's idiosyncratic terms are difficult to pin down with absolute certainty, but these are the most likely explanations.

BAIL
A sixteenth-century term for a crossbar used to hold something in place (e.g. the top of a gate). (See *wicket*.)

BAT
From the Old English word *batt*, meaning 'club, stick or staff'.

CHINAMAN
The left-arm bowler's off-break to a right-hander. An unorthodox delivery that was politically incorrectly associated with the stereotype of a cunning 'Chinaman'.

CREASE

Before the introduction of painted white lines in the second half of the nineteenth century, the crease was a furrow cut in the turf.

GOOGLY

From the notion that the ball so mystified batsmen that it made their eyes 'goggle' or (in some dialects) 'google'.

GULLY

The channel between the slips and point.

HAT-TRICK

On having achieved the feat of taking three wickets in successive balls, the bowler would be rewarded with a new hat or a hat would be passed among spectators for a collection.

MAIDEN OVER

'Maiden' in the sense of unproductive (e.g. a maiden aunt).

POINT

Originally called 'point of the bat', the fielder in this position was almost within reach of the end of the striker's bat.

POPPING CREASE

To complete a 'notch' or run, batsmen originally had to place their bat in a shallow hole in front of the stumps. If the wicketkeeper or fieldsman popped the ball into the hole before the batsman could reach it, the latter was deemed run out. Hand injuries to fielders colliding with the bat in the popping hole eventually led to the modern demarcation line.

WICKET

A wicket gate is often part of, or next to, a larger gate built into a fence or wall. Shepherds playing a primitive form of the game on the downs probably used the gate of a sheep pen as a 'wicket'.

YORKER

'York' and 'Yorkshire' have historical slang connotations of sharp practice. To be 'yorked' was to be deceived – the fate of any batsman dismissed by a yorker.

SELECTED FACTS
AND FIGURES

· ·

TEST CRICKET

FIRST BATSMEN TO SCORE INNINGS OF 100, 200, 300 AND 400 IN TESTS

165* C. Bannerman (AU)
Australia v England (Melbourne), 1877

211 W. L. Murdoch (AU)
England v Australia (The Oval), 1884

325 A. Sandham (ENG)
West Indies v England (Jamaica), 1930

400 n.o. B. Lara (WI)
West Indies v England (Antigua), 2004

* Since this was in the first ever Test match, he was also the first
man to score a Test hundred on debut.

HIGHEST SCORE ON TEST DEBUT
287 R. E. Foster (ENG)
Australia v England (Sydney), 1903

FIRST BOWLERS TO TAKE 100 TO 800 TEST WICKETS

100 (118)	J. Briggs (ENG)	1895
200 (216)	C. V. Grimmett (AU)	1936
300 (307)	F. S. Trueman (ENG)	1964
400 (431)	R. J. Hadlee (NZ)	1990
500 (519)	C. Walsh (WI)	2001
600 (708)	S. Warne (AU)	2005
700 (708)	S. Warne (AU)	2006
800 (800)	M. Muralitharan (SL)	2010

FIRST TEST HAT-TRICK
F. R. Spofforth (AU)
Australia v England (Melbourne), 1879

FIRST TEST HAT-TRICK IN EACH INNINGS
T. J. Matthews (AU)
Australia v South Africa (Old Trafford), 1912

FIRST BOWLER TO TAKE TEN WICKETS IN A TEST INNINGS
Jim Laker (ENG) 10 for 53
England v Australia (Old Trafford), 1956

HIGHEST TEST INNINGS TOTAL
952 for 6
by Sri Lanka v India (Colombo), 1997

LOWEST TEST INNINGS TOTAL

26

by New Zealand v England (Auckland), 1955

ONE-DAY INTERNATIONALS

FIRST PLAYER TO SCORE A HUNDRED IN AN ODI

Dennis Amiss (ENG) 103*

England v Australia (Old Trafford), 1972

* ODI debut

FIRST PLAYER TO SCORE 200 IN AN ODI

Sachin Tendulkar (I) 200 n.o.

India v South Africa (Gwalior), 2010

FIRST BOWLER TO TAKE 5 WICKETS IN AN ODI

Dennis Lillee (AU) 5 for 34

Australia v Pakistan (Leeds), 1975

TWENTY20 INTERNATIONALS

FIRST PLAYER TO SCORE A HUNDRED

Chris Gayle (WI) 117

South Africa v West Indies (Johannesburg), 2007

FIRST BOWLER TO TAKE 5 WICKETS
Umar Gul (P) 5 for 6*
Pakistan v New Zealand (the Oval), 2009
* Umar Gul also took 5 for 6 against South Africa in 2013

FIRST-CLASS CRICKET

MOST RUNS IN A CAREER
Jack Hobbs (Surrey/England, 1905–34) 61,760 (av. 50.70)

MOST CENTURIES IN A CAREER
Jack Hobbs (Surrey/England, 1905–34) 199

MOST WICKETS IN A CAREER
Wilfred Rhodes (Yorkshire/England, 1898–1930)
 4,204 (av. 16.72)

MOST WICKETKEEPING DISMISSALS
Bob Taylor (Derbyshire/England, 1960–88)
1,649 (ct. 1,473; st. 176)

HIGHEST INDIVIDUAL INNINGS
Brian Lara (Warwickshire/WI) 501 n.o.
Warwickshire v Durham, 1994

BEST INDIVIDUAL BOWLING ANALYSIS
Hedley Verity (Yorkshire/England) 10 for 10
Yorkshire v Nottinghamshire, 1932

MOST FIRST-CLASS HAT-TRICKS
Doug Wright (Kent/England, 1932–57) 7

WOMEN'S TEST MATCHES

MOST RUNS IN A TEST CAREER
Jan Brittin (ENG), 1979-98 1,935 (av. 49.61)

MOST WICKETS IN A TEST CAREER
Mary Duggan (ENG), 1949-63 77 (av. 13.49)

FIRST PLAYER TO SCORE 100 IN A TEST
Myrtle Maclagan (ENG) 119
Australia v England (Sydney), 1935

FIRST PLAYER TO SCORE 200 IN A TEST
Kirsty Flavell (NZ) 204
England v New Zealand (Scarborough), 1996

WOMEN'S ONE-DAY INTERNATIONALS

HIGHEST INDIVIDUAL INNINGS
Belinda Clark (AU) 229 n.o.
Australia v Denmark (Mumbai), 1997

BEST INDIVIDUAL BOWLING ANALYSIS

Sajjida Shah (P) 7 for 4

Japan v Pakistan (Amsterdam), 2003

WOMEN'S TWENTY20 INTERNATIONALS

FIRST PLAYER TO SCORE A HUNDRED

Deandra Dottin (WI) 112 n.o.

West Indies v South Africa (St Kitts), 2010

FIRST BOWLER TO TAKE 6 WICKETS IN AN INNINGS

Amy Satterthwaite (NZ) 6 for 17

England v New Zealand (Taunton), 2007

IT'S A FACT!

In 1981, a woman from Wolverhampton was granted a divorce on the grounds of her husband's unreasonable behaviour. She told the court he was 'cricket mad'.

RESOURCES

WEBSITES

www.ecb.co.uk
Official website for the England and Wales Cricket Board, with information on every aspect of the game in the UK, including cricket for the disabled.

www.espncricinfo.com
The most comprehensive online source of information about cricket worldwide, with stats, scores, match reports, player profiles and countless other features.

www.icc-cricket.com/team-rankings
World team rankings for Tests, international ODIs and Twenty20s, plus player rankings for batting and bowling (male and female).

www.lords.org
Everything you need to know about cricket's historical headquarters, from the MCC Academy to the laws of the game.

www.cricketweb.net
A less reverential though nonetheless enthusiastic website, with fantasy cricket, lively blogs and a veritable library of book reviews.

BOOKS

Cricket has an inexhaustible library and these are just a few of the books worth 'borrowing':

Wisden Cricketers' Almanack (published annually by Bloomsbury)

Playfair Cricket Annual (published annually by Headline)

Beyond a Boundary: James, C. L. R. (Hutchinson, 1963)

The Art of Captaincy: Brearley, Mike (Pan Macmillan, 1985)

Coming Back to Me: Trescothick, Marcus (HarperCollins, 2008)

Rain Men: Madness of Cricket: Berkmann, Marcus (Little, Brown, 1995)

A Lot of Hard Yakka: Hughes, Simon (Headline, 1998)

Brightly Fades the Don: Fingleton, Jack (Collins, 1949)

War Minus the Shooting: Marqusee, Mike (William Heinemann, 1996)

Penguins Stopped Play: Eleven Village Cricketers Take on the World: Thompson, Harry (John Murray, 2006)

MAGAZINES

The Cricketer (monthly) – Has been covering cricket in depth since 1921

All Out Cricket (monthly) – News, views and reviews

The Cricket Paper – The UK's only weekly newspaper dedicated to the sport

MUSEUMS

Several of the first-class counties have their own museums, and there are other cricket museums around the world. The leading museum in the UK is at the game's HQ:

MCC Museum
Lord's Cricket Ground, St John's Wood Road, London NW8 8QN
020 7616 8658

www.mccmuseum@mcc.org.uk
Founded in 1953, the museum's impressive collection includes the original Ashes urn. Open throughout the year, it forms part of the Lord's tour.

If you're interested in finding out more about our books,
find us on Facebook at **Summersdale Publishers**
and follow us on Twitter at **@Summersdale**

www.summersdale.com